The Cult of Dissatisfaction

Empowering unhappy professional women wanting change.

JACQUI BRAUMAN

ISBN:0994514654
ISBN-13: 978-0-9945146-5-3

A Master Wordsmith Book

THE
MASTER WORDSMITH

Masterpiece Services for Entrepreneur Authors

www.themasterwordsmith.com

DEDICATION

To my husband, who tolerates my dreams and puts up
with my workaholism. It's all for you.

CONTENTS

INTRODUCTION

The self-help industry is booming, but if you're anything like me, then you don't go for all the "rah-rah" and fist pumping stuff. And I certainly don't want to hold anyone's hand or hug any strangers. That might be helpful for you, but it seems too fluffy and temporary for me. But there are a few good messages in all the fluff, such as "if you want things to change, then you need to change", "nothing ventured, nothing gained", and to a degree, "you choose the life you get".

Everyone wants to change, but day in and day out we can't make ourselves do it—or even make a decision to try! Part of this struggle to decide to make a change lies in having to break free from the general malaise of dissatisfaction that seems to permeate every Western society now. It's frankly easier to be dissatisfied than to change. People are more fond of complaining, whining and whinging about their plight than they are willing to do anything about it. This trend of negativity keeps them down, and keeps them from taking control and achieving what they truly want. And what "they" do tends to become what "we" do, because we're part of the same society together and it's often easier just to go along.

Behind the whinging and whining, though, seems to be a deeper dissatisfaction with society and our individual and collective circumstances, among both sexes. We seem to know deep down that life wasn't supposed to be this hard. Education and work life are still set up for the industrial revolution and the labour movement. But no-one can truly get ahead working 9 to 5 these days, with only one income per family. The labour unions helped in times gone past, for our grandparents, but they don't now. That generational way of thinking no longer applies. We seem to all be struggling against it, feeling the dissatisfaction of dual-income families working longer and longer hours, juggling more and more in life. We tell ourselves that life is not meant to be like this, but when we look around and interact with our peers, we don't see much to make us believe it.

When we are surrounded by negativity, with our friends and colleagues, in the media and on the news, it is like being brain-washed by a cult. This dissatisfaction that others express about their lives, and the constant striving for material possessions and competing for the latest and greatest consumables, are all external contributors to our dissatisfaction.

We need to wake up from the brain-washing, so that we can take back control of our own lives. We can create what we want for ourselves, if we stop letting the negativity suck us back into the quicksand of dissatisfaction. This book will outline several ways of extracting ourselves from the external factors that cause our dissatisfaction.

But let's face it; much of our dissatisfaction is also caused by our own internal mental baggage. This is absolutely the case when contemplating a big change in our life. Doubt, fear, comparison with others, and the self-worth struggles that we go through all hold us back from change.

I'm not sure if men go through the same struggles, but I think women tend to be far more insecure. We doubt our capabilities, we doubt that our experience is valuable, we doubt that we have anything to offer, we doubt that we will be taken seriously. This doubt often leads to dissatisfaction with ourselves as women, with aspects of our home lives, our careers, and with society in general.

Women are also more likely to let fear get in our way than men. We become paralysed with fear. We turn away from our opportunities because of our fear. It could be fear of being judged by others, fear of being compared and falling short, or fear of success. There are many reasons why we could be fearful, but none of them are justified. We are our own worst critics, but if we reach out and talk through our fears with other women, we will find a very supportive community that can help us see how baseless and powerless our fears really are.

The comparisons we make between ourselves and others are often the worst mental merry-go-round that we could get on. When we compare ourselves with other women, and let the doubt and fear take control, our self-worth plummets. It is a vicious cycle. Once we doubt our capabilities, and we feel less worthy, we spiral downwards until our self-confidence is crushed on the ground like a snail that has ventured out onto the pavement. We are dissatisfied and out of control.

We cannot bring ourselves to pursue our goals, or bring about change, when our confidence and self-esteem has plummeted. So instead, our old patterns include calling up those old friends to have a catch-up meal, listening to their complaints and gripes, and succumbing to the whinging and whining trend on our own minds, once again. We need strategies to make sure we don't begin the downward cycle, so that our self-worth remains realistic and based on our actual worth.

This book is for women who are tired of letting dissatisfaction control them, and want to take that control back themselves. It explores a lot of the mental battles, barriers, decisions and triumphs that I have faced as a lawyer and a business owner. It also explores my own dissatisfaction with my career, and the legal industry, and my journey to change that. My battles with dissatisfaction and its symptoms are detailed here, and I hope that you can relate, so that your decision to deal with it and change for yourself will be easier. I am nowhere near perfect, but I have begun taking back my own control. My biggest hope is that you can learn from the struggles that I outline here.

This book is set up in three parts. In Part One, I will explore the cult of dissatisfaction deeply, digging into external and cultural factors that contribute to feelings of dissatisfaction. In Part Two you will learn the internal symptoms of dissatisfaction, and what can cause and contribute to dissatisfaction within yourself. In Part Three, you will learn what to do about dissatisfaction, how to take control back and make a change. This book does not have to be read in order, or in its entirety. I want you to read it such that you will get the most out of it. If you want to jump right to Part Two or Three, or to a specific chapter that grabs your attention, feel free.

I wish you well, and hope that you enjoy this book. If you do, I would love if you came to my blog at www.haveitall.net.au and tell me what you've learnt, or what else I can help you with. Having it all is about your individual happiness, and I want you to be happy, because you are a professional woman living in the early twenty-first century, just as I am. Or you can contact me directly at jacqui@haveitall.net.au. Thanks for reading!

'Once upon a time you were a little girl with big dreams that you promised you'd make real one day. Don't disappoint yourself.'
-Unknown

PART ONE: DISSATISFACTION

A cult does not have to be a system of religion or devotion. Cults are also defined as *"a person or thing that is popular or fashionable among a particular group or section of society"*. In other words, a fad, a vogue, or a fashion. At the moment, it seems fashionable to be miserable and to complain. Dissatisfaction has become a cult.

So many people get a strange kind of pleasure out of talking about how miserable their lives are. They complain about their jobs, their wage, their marriage, their children, their material possessions or lack thereof. They seem to compete with each other about who has the most miserable life. Winning that competition doesn't make them feel good, because they're still miserable, but it makes them feel better than whoever they're talking to. Apparently they've convinced themselves that's the best they can hope for.

This is the cult of dissatisfaction. It has pervaded all levels of our society, and appears to stem from a deep dissatisfaction with the structure of our society, including the way we work and the way the genders relate to each other. We are dissatisfied with not being able to get ahead, with not being able to live the lives we want, and with not meeting our own expectations. We are dissatisfied with how much we have to work, with how little we earn, and with how little we are appreciated. We are dissatisfied with how we are treated, with how others are treated, with how little things actually change, and with our poor political representation. We are just not happy with much at the moment!

Part One will explore this deep dissatisfaction. We start with a look at cultural dissatisfaction, and how the Western culture is dissatisfied with having to work all our lives to be able to "live" in retirement. Then we explore relationship and political dissatisfaction, and the increasing attitude of entitlement amongst the dissatisfied. Another aspect of dissatisfaction we'll talk about is the feeling that we are doing what's expected of us, instead of what we were really meant to do, or what we enjoy to do. This includes doing what we think people expect of us, as well as fitting into stereotypes, and having to restrain ourselves to be politically correct. Finally, since this book is primarily for professional women, we'll explore the dissatisfaction that we are living and working in a man's world still.

Because its goal is to help you understand the whole dissatisfaction cult, Part One isn't the happiest section. To be honest Part One will probably leave you feeling more dissatisfied than you were when you opened this book. But as I explained in the introduction, you can feel free to jump around in this book. If you need to do so immediately, proceed to the uplifting Part Three to find out how to change your circumstances.

'Change occurs in direct proportion to dissatisfaction, but dissatisfaction never changes.'

- Douglas Horton

1 CULTURAL DISSATISFACTION

Arguably, our individual dissatisfaction begins because of our society. Whilst current Western society has given us more options than ever before, happiness is more fleeting than ever. More than ever, we are trying to "keep up with the Joneses" and we want more and more material possessions. But at the same time, living is getting more and more expensive, and we are so busy making a living that we are forgetting to live.

Most women that I meet these days, especially trying to have both a career and a family, are *exhausted*. We were told by our feminist mothers that we could have it all—a high-paid career, happy children, a beautiful home, and a loving marriage. But what about our own happiness along the way? Have we really been taught that we can *only* be happy if we can successfully juggle all these things? What if we don't want them all? Or what if we want something outside of all of them? And even if we do want some or all of those things, how long do we have to work to get them? Our Western culture has sold us the myth that if we lead a safe, mediocre life, work in the same job for 40 years and pay off a mortgage, then we will retire to enjoy our later years. But our later years keep getting later, and later, and later, as we see our peers (or our parents) working for years past when they planned to retire.

We are dissatisfied that this is all life seems to holds for us. We know that we have a purpose that's more than just working to survive. Our dissatisfaction with our situations extends to our loved ones, society and 'the system'. These are some of the external causes of dissatisfaction, and the traps we can fall into if we succumb to the cult.

Sold the Myth

In most Western or first-world countries, we have grown up in the post-industrialised culture that tells us to go to school, work all our lives, and then retire. We try to do our best at school, so we can get the best job we can. We take few risks outside this formula. We work all our lives, pay off a mortgage, get married and have some children, and put some money away into superannuation. Apparently, this is the great Australian dream. It's the same in other first-world countries. This is the way society is programming us to live. But in reality, it's a myth that this programmed lifestyle makes a successful life, and we become dissatisfied because we know it is a myth.

Despite the majority of people following this program of working all their lives to retire at 65 years of age, it is not a formula for financial success. They work and work and work all their lives, but then cannot support themselves in retirement. The money they thought would be there to support them never shows up or grows enough to do it. The majority of Australians (over 80% according to the National Commission of Audit) are currently, and this percentage is projected to remain consistent for 40 years, reliant on the government pension in some form or another during retirement.

We've been sold a myth. We are capable of far more, and the disappointment we often feel comes from restricting ourselves to the very program society wants us to follow. We delay living our lives until we retire, and put off doing what we really want to do in life until we're past our prime, but then look ahead and see ourselves working for another twenty or thirty years, without any change, and with no guarantee we'll be successful or supported at the end. This makes us miserable!

But is this kind of life really necessary for success? I don't think so, and neither does Tim Ferriss, the author of *The Four-Hour Work Week* and one of the first pioneers of lifestyle design. He writes:

Life doesn't have to be damn hard. It really doesn't. Most people, my past self included, have spent too much time convincing themselves that life has to be hard, a resignation to the 9-to-5 drudgery in exchange for (sometimes) relaxing weekends and the occasional keep-it-short-or-get-fired vacation.

I don't think most people have accepted the status quo. If they had, people like Tim Ferriss wouldn't have an audience. Instead, I believe that most people are dissatisfied with the status quo *but don't know what to do about it*. Women in their twenties, thirties and forties have not reached resignation yet - they are still thrashing about in their minds, seeking some alternative, and finding mostly frustration. By fifty or sixty, many women have either accepted their fate or just stopped caring. This is not good enough.

We don't have to repeat history through the

generations. Just because your parents lived in a small town, got married at 17, took a "safe" apprenticeship instead of university, and worked a 9-to-5 for 40 years, that doesn't mean you have to do the same. Having it all is about your own happiness, not about doing what others do—or what you think they expect of you.

You have choices and, with the growth of the web, your choices have compounded exponentially. You control your life and what happens in it, and, once you realise that fully, you give yourself room to grow, experiment, and begin designing the life of your dreams without dissatisfaction.

Relationships/Politics

Two more aspects of our modern lives that fall victim to the cult of dissatisfaction are our personal, intimate relationships, and politics. These two things may seem like they have nothing to do with each other, but in this context they work very similarly. As our dissatisfaction with our lives and our situation overflows to affect the world around us, we often blame others for how we feel. Our partners and our governments both receive lots of this blame.

Our most intimate relationships cop a lot of blame for our dissatisfaction with ourselves and how our lives are turning out. Blaming our loved ones for our own issues is backward and unfair, because we are in control of most of our decisions.

Dissatisfaction with our political representatives, and the performance of government, has also never been higher. The standard of living has been increasing for decades, but that doesn't mean that we are satisfied with it—especially since we aren't often the ones to see the effects of that increase in our own lives. Our dissatisfaction with what we earn, how much we work, how much we have to pay for education and medical treatment, and the general cost of living needs a target. We rarely want to blame ourselves for our lives, so we look to "the system" and to the government to lay blame.

Not only do we blame the government for our general dissatisfaction with our lives, but we also get frustrated at the lack of representation for our particular views—especially when our views seem to be years ahead of our representatives' views, or our needs don't fit into their agendas. Where are the strong policies on climate change? What political party will finally step up and make same-sex marriage legal? They all spout support for small business and job growth, but when will there actually be some policies that help small business practically? They all have views on reforms for child care, but no one has implemented a solution that works. If you don't share these objections with me, I bet you have others of your own.

This dissatisfaction with our political representatives often turns into impatience and frustration, which historically has led to change in the past but if we do not drive the efforts to change things now, what will change going forward? Nothing.

The media plays a big role in our dissatisfaction with both our personal relationships and with government. The media loves to report negative stories - negativity about relationships, domestic violence in relationships, the negative effects on children, etc - then we have a skewed view that this situation is the majority of relationships and not the exception. Likewise, the media loves to beat up irrelevant political stories, and focus on issues that aren't actually important most of the time. The media rarely provides a full, fair story. And more and more news outlets have their own agenda that they are pushing, so we need to be conscious enough of this to be able to view the stories for what they are. I consume as little news these days as I can, and I suggest that you do the same.

So once you can start recognising that you are dissatisfied with your life, you can be conscious not to blame your spouse or other family members. You can understand that your dissatisfaction and negativity often increases the more media you consume. You may realise that the system will remain the same unless you get involved in some way, and if you're not trying to be part of the change, you can learn to be careful about laying blame. These are choices that you have control over, to extract yourself from the cult of dissatisfaction.

The first principle is that you must not fool yourself - and you are the easiest person to fool.'

- *Richard Feynman*

Entitlement

There are many who believe that they should get something for nothing, or that the government should look after them, or that they should advance in life faster than they have for their mediocre effort. Their dissatisfaction, and quite often anger at the world, is generated from the fact that they believe they are not getting what they deserve. Living a life in the cult of dissatisfaction due to an attitude of entitlement is exhausting and miserable.

Those with an entitlement attitude believe that they have done enough to deserve great things. Then they are dissatisfied that their expectations aren't met, and they fall into the cult of dissatisfaction with others. Once the cult of dissatisfaction sucks them down, they commiserate with others and whinge about the results they are getting in life. They blame others. They don't look at themselves and take control of their lives, and keep pushing until they get what they want. They stop, they wait for someone or something else to give them their deserts, and sadly, they usually lead a dissatisfying life full of regret.

There is also a lot of entitlement-related apathy in various industries. When people believe that their job or contribution doesn't matter, they become used to simply showing up and getting a paycheque. The longer this goes on, the less work they want to do and the more money they want for putting up with work they don't care about. This creates an attitude of dissatisfaction and entitlement. The sense of entitlement - that they are worth more, and therefore deserve better than what they have - is a form of selfishness, as Ryan Holiday says, that drives people to laziness and lethargy. They stop trying.

An entitlement attitude can go further than making us lethargic and lazy; it can lead to selfish and negative thinking. In intimate relationships, an entitlement attitude might result in someone cheating, justifying an affair rather than working to build a relationship that meets their needs. In regards to our financial obligations, someone's friends may have all the latest gadgets and a huge flat screen TV, so they go out and buy the same because they 'deserve it' even if they actually can't afford it. They are often unable to delay this kind of gratification, which causes an accumulation of debt.

Those with a sense of entitlement tend to lack gratitude for what they have, and struggle to take personal responsibility for their lives and situations. This leads back to further dissatisfaction and more blaming of others.

Unfortunately, entitlement often starts in childhood. Many children are raised to believe that they are entitled to something—possibly through viewing and learning entitled attitudes from their parents. By the time they grow up, it's hard to snap out of long-learned behaviour. Even if entitlement was learned later in life, it's still tough to overcome.

It's not impossible, though. "Wants" and "needs" can be redefined, and gratitude journalling and learning financial responsibility can all help. Most importantly, we need to start taking personal responsibility for where we are in life and the choices we have made. Remember, no one owes us anything. Accept that our past has created us into the person we are, with our many strengths and unique qualities, and use what we have to achieve what we want in life.

The unhappiest people in this world are those who care the most about what other people think.'

- C. Joybell C.

2 DOING WHAT'S EXPECTED

Perhaps the biggest tragedy in our lives is that we can pass years doing things we don't want to do, to impress people we don't really care about. Decades disappear whilst we mindlessly continue doing what we think society wants us to do, living our lives on other people's terms.

Often we hold ourselves back just because of what we think other people expect of us. If we do mention a dream or goal, if we get the slightest negative or even ambiguous response, we will often give up. Because others, society, our parents, our partners, all think we should live a certain way or do certain things, we do what they expect or approve of just to keep them happy.

This often means staying within our culture, our

economic means, and our stereotypes. Were you told as a child "don't get too big for your boots"? The tall poppy syndrome is alive and well in Australia: if we step up and out of the role we're expected to fill, we can be "cut down to size". If we become more financially successful than our peers, we can be ostracised. If we don't fit within the expected female stereotype, we are undermined. .

Under these limiting expectations, we can feel trapped and dissatisfied, wishing to break free, to do what we know we can, or even try something that we want to try. Yet when we do see other brave women break free of what's expected of them, we see them often have to leave their family behind, or deal with relationships and reputations so damaged that they must forge a new path alone. Choosing to do something other than what the world expects of us can be a scary choice. Either way we risk something big.

What Other People Think

People nearly always make choices based on other people. Women in particular can be very self-conscious and fearful of what other people think of us, particularly other women. We are our own worst enemies. We don't do certain things, like work out, because we are worried about how we will look. We often make decisions about what we should eat or wear based on what we *think* others will think of us. We also do the same thing when it comes to big decisions in our lives, such as making a career choice, often to our own detriment. We are more concerned about what other people will think of us, than actually doing what is best for us.

I have wanted to be a writer since I could pick up a book. "Read a book" was one of my first phrases, as I would toddle after my mother, holding up the latest book that I wanted her to read to me. I memorised books as a child, and I would "read" to myself. If I couldn't remember the story, then I would make the story up from the pictures.

I wrote my own picture books and novels in primary school, I entered writing competitions and won occasionally. I submitted my first manuscript to Penguin publishing and got rejected as a ten-year-old. But I kept writing. I was determined. Until one day I wasn't anymore. Somewhere along the way, I let my dream go. Why did that determination disappear?

Somewhere along the way, I picked up the concept of the "starving artist". I didn't call it that, but I learnt, or heard from society and culture, that I couldn't make money from art, or writing. So I decided briefly that I would be a journalist. At least that way I could still write. But this went out the window as well, as my marks got better throughout high school and I was the top of my class (but one) when I graduated.

I let go of my dream for the prestige of chasing a good income. I let it go because I thought someone with the marks I got became either a doctor or a lawyer. So I did law, forgot about writing, and let my dream fall away.

For the last fifteen years, I have been pushing myself in my industry, achieving higher and higher legal qualifications, and burning the candle at both ends to meet my clients' needs. I've been chasing that higher income and greater prestige that I thought my grades had destined me for. And I've learned: I'm not happy as a lawyer.

I do enjoy helping people, but the law is rarely fulfilling for me. I am achieving for the sake of achieving. I am striving because my colleagues and the industry expect it. I am watching them watching me, judging me, and I am judging myself. As I said at the beginning, I have been doing a job I don't want to be doing for a long time, and I have been doing it to impress people that I don't really know or care about. (And of course, I earn about a third of what a male with my qualifications would earn!)

I now know that staying a lawyer isn't in my long-term future. But fighting through the expectations of the world to realise that wasn't easy. Caged in by my self-judgment, believing that I had to prove myself to other people, and feeding my own anxiety, I spent years being restless and dissatisfied. To overcome my perceived flaws and to fight off that dissatisfaction, I became a control freak. I tried to control my body, my emotions, my environment, and even the people around me.

It was bad. I needed pens to sit in a certain way in a certain place. I needed the dishwasher packed in a certain order. I needed the toilet paper to roll in a certain way. I needed the shoes at the door to line up in pairs. I needed my keys and my phone in specific little pockets in my bag. I couldn't have anything on the floor - *nothing* could be on the floor, ever. Because. I. Was. In. Control.

Can you relate?

None of these controlling behaviours allow us to stop and realise that we are actually in control of our own lives. Our own decisions put us in the positions we are in, even if we made those decisions to please other people. We had the control to get ourselves into this mess, we have the control to get ourselves out.

There may not be a quick fix to getting out of the deep holes we've dug ourselves into, but we can certainly stop digging!

I was forced to accept that I chose to do law for the wrong reasons. It was my decision, and it has certainly shaped me into the person that I am today. That is not entirely a bad thing--when I wasn't freaking out with anxiety and starving myself into a "hangry" state, I became a very good lawyer. I'm proud of that. But what I do for the next couple of decades is my decision, too. I am in control of who I'm going to be in the future, and it doesn't have to be the person I was for the last fifteen years. I hope you can find this realisation for yourself!

Stereotypes

Here's an unpopular opinion: gender roles aren't all bad. Really. In fact, they are not necessarily either positive or negative. But they are oversimplified and can be inaccurate. Gender roles are generalisations of male and female attributes that aren't actually related to a person's gender at all, because males can display what are typically "feminine" traits and women can display typically "masculine" traits. It is a mistake to define characteristics as masculine or feminine anymore, like two extreme opposites, when really they are just character traits. Since each person has individual desires, thoughts, goals and feelings, regardless of their gender, gender stereotypes can be incredibly simplistic short-sighted. Here are a few that are particularly outdated:

- women are supposed to have 'clean jobs' like secretaries, teachers and librarians
- women are nurses, but not doctors
- women are not as strong as men
- women are supposed to make less money than men
- women are quieter than men and are not meant to speak out
- women are supposed to be submissive and be told what to do
- women are supposed to cook and do the housework
- women are responsible for raising children
- women do not have technical skills and are not good at 'hands on' projects
- women love to sing and dance, and
- women are meant to be the damsel in distress, never the hero.

Some women do fit these stereotypes. But many

women don't. Some fit a few of them but not others. Some choose to avoid most of them but keep one or two. Some women find fulfillment in traditional roles, whilst others find their fulfillment in non-traditional ones. The point is, all women can choose their roles based on their individual personalities. No woman should be judged for their choices. On top of that, there are men who choose to fit some of these feminine stereotypes—some of the strongest men I've met are stay-at-home dads.

Like Emma Watson says, gender is a spectrum, not black or white, not two sets of opposing ideals. Why do we subscribe to the so-called masculine and feminine characteristics? We are all various shades of grey, and should not be characterised by our genders.

Gone are the days when women needed to fit into a stereotypical role, however we also need to be aware that stereotypes still exist. Both men and women will subconsciously try to fit us into stereotypes. But we cannot let it hold us back, or define who we are. Be yourself, prove stereotypes wrong.

For example: I am a highly educated professional woman, yet I earn far less than my male counterparts. I still do most of the cooking at home, and most of the internal housework. I hate singing and dancing, I love maths, I love video games, I hate flirting and try to be as asexual as possible most of the time, I am certainly not a damsel in distress - I am not timid and scared, and I am strong and love sport. I also use swear words, and I have a firm hand shake. I am sure I will be judged for all of these things, and many people will not know how to categorise me. But we need to get out of the need to categorise people, and take people for whom they are regardless of gender.

I have shied away from female stereotypes, or being stereotyped myself, as much as I can. I believe that I got this from my mother, who grew up with four brothers and is a strong feminist. As a child, she wouldn't dress me in pink, but instead I wore neutral colours and usually pants. I was climbing trees, reading books, and playing with Transformers. Mum did try to give me Barbie dolls, but I used to cut their hair and rip their heads off, so she gave up.

As much as my mother tried to give me as gender-neutral a childhood as possible, the school system can't help but use stereotypes. I was a very self-aware child, and became conscious of how I was different to the other little girls. But I continued to play with the boys, and "boss them around" for a couple of years, until I was about seven or eight years old. Then it wasn't as acceptable, for some reason. Apparently, being a bossy little girl wasn't a desirable trait, so that was quickly squashed out of me and I became far more meek and stand-offish.

I cannot say whether this was fair to me or not, or who I would have been if society did not stereotype little girls and boys, and was far more accepting of them as individuals. I recently listened to a very interesting TEDx Talk by Christopher Bell entitled "Bring On Female Superheroes!" and I applaud him for it. If there were more males that embraced feminism on behalf of their daughters, then we might leave stereotypes behind entirely one day.

That being said, as a woman, I also have advantages working in a male-dominated industry that I can utilise. I am soft spoken, so I demand attention when I speak. I am polite and I smile a lot, but that doesn't mean I am meek or weak. I also believe that I am less threatening and intimidating for my clients, so I make clients far more comfortable. Be aware of what stereotypes you are breaking, and which you can embrace to your advantage. Don't be dissatisfied because you feel you have to comply with a stereotype - you don't. Remember, you don't have to be worried about what other people think of you.

More importantly, if you are dissatisfied by being pigeon-holed by a stereotype, then make sure you don't do it to other women. Let go of the stereotypes that you apply to others, and stop forcing certain roles and traits on your fellow women. Often we are our own worst enemies. When we stereotype our own female colleagues and community members, we are discounting some amazing resources, supporters, and collaborators.

Political Correctness

Political correctness is supposed to be fair, but in reality it can be stifling. It's supposed to make sure we avoid any forms of expression that exclude, marginalise, or insult specific groups of people (especially those who have already been socially disadvantaged or discriminated against). But lately, what it really seems to be doing is labelling, vilifying, and punishing people by taking their comments out of context or blowing them out of proportion.

I don't support marginalising or insulting any group through generalisations, stereotypes, racism or anything else. As a woman, I am often the subject of broad generalisations and harmful stereotypes. But I believe that the fear of online trolls and mass media turning on us has made even the most reasonable of us scared to express an opinion. We are afraid that our own views will be labelled as racist, sexist, homophobic, generally insensitive, or otherwise worthy of judgment—even when we meant nothing of the kind. We are afraid that if we don't conform with the majority opinion (which is not always the wisest place to be) we will be ostracised. We are scared that our thoughts could be taken out of context and used to make us look ridiculous or despicable. We have seen women in the media in Australia driven to depression and suicide due to trolls. We're afraid of being bullied, shouted down, called names, and having our character questioned or insulted simply for expressing a different opinion. Feeling like we have to go along with the crowd when the crowd's opinion is different from our own can lead to intense dissatisfaction.

Another way that women feel repressed by political correctness is when we want to fit in with our peers. We want to be part of a team at work, or a group that is predominantly male. Yet, to do so, we often accept a degrading comment disguised as a joke, and laugh it off with the others. We don't want to say anything or pull someone up for being politically incorrect, because we don't want to look like a bitch if we complain.

To fit in to a team of predominantly executive males, in a very masculine industry, I quite often laughed off jokes from my male colleagues that the only way I was achieving success was by offering sexual favours. The men didn't like that I could get results that they couldn't, so they had to put it down to me offering the one thing that they didn't have - my vagina! In reality, I was just far more skilled than they were at developing relationships and understanding what the other party wanted so we could achieve a positive outcome for both. But I had to joke along, each time I got back from another successful meeting and my achievements were degraded. I wanted to fit in, so I didn't want to tell them off for doing it, particularly as my boss was one of the main ring-leaders. This is explored more thoroughly in the next chapter about living in a man's world.

So by feeling like we need to be politically correct, is yet another way that we restrict who we are to conform with society, with what other people expect, with stereotypes, and with our fear of rejection. Our dissatisfaction arises from our inability or fear to express ourselves, and our apparent need to be what society wants us to be. This can really only be dealt with through finding a deep acceptance of ourselves and the confidence that that can bring. Finding people who truly value us and lift our confidence is the beginning, and surrounding ourselves with supportive women is the first step.

Equality of opportunity is freedom, but equality of outcome is repression.'

- Dick Feagler

3 A MAN'S WORLD

In our world of political correctness, I almost feel sorry for the middle-aged white males in our society. Almost. Because they are the most privileged group in society, and often have the best assumptions made about them automatically, they tend to struggle the most with changing the way they talk and think. But that doesn't make those changes any less necessary, and the middle-aged white men's unwillingness to embrace those changes really makes it impossible for me to actually pity them. There cannot be reverse sexism or racism, because by definition the oppressed cannot be the oppressors. Middle-aged white men are just feeling pressure to change, and they don't like it. Tough.

The problem is, whilst we are far more aware of

minority groups now, our culture has already been established for hundreds of years by and for the middle-aged white males of the world. How business works, how the law works, and even how we interact on a day-to-day basis through our customs and speech was all established by middle-aged white males.

Our culture, with its emphasis on self-reliance and independence - qualities deemed especially important for men - has reinforced the message that having needs is bad and wrong. Even in this age of greater vulnerability and authenticity, any sign of softness in business is generally frowned upon.

So how does a modern woman survive in a culture that has been established by and for middle-aged white men? How does she retain femininity and excel on her own terms, instead of putting on a mask and turning into someone else? Quite often the transformation we need to make to succeed in a traditional male industry is dissatisfying.

These are questions I constantly struggle with, and I often wonder if I have lost my true self after having worn the mask for so many years. I don my armour every morning and pretend to be someone else, so that I can survive in the man's world. But over time, the armour gets harder and harder to remove at the end of the day. It is dissatisfying and exhausting trying to be someone else all the time, and it's a little frightening how easily I can stay in that persona after all these years.

Equality and Equity

I've never considered myself a feminist. I have always thought of feminists as the generations of women gone by, who made it possible for us to vote and be highly educated and work in a broad range of industries even after we are married. Feminism also engenders an aggression (even man-hating) that I don't feel, and I don't believe is needed anymore. I consider myself an equalist - I believe everyone should have the same rights and opportunities, regardless of gender, race or age. I also believe in treating everyone equitably, or with a deep moral fairness.

There is a difference between equality and equity, and it's often about finding that balance as to which to apply when. Equality is treating everyone the same. It aims to promote fairness, but treating everyone equally assumes everyone has the same skills and needs. Equity is not treating everyone the same, but instead is giving each person what he or she individually needs to succeed.

Equality versus equity in the gender argument is difficult. As a woman, I would prefer to be treated equally to my male peers, and to be able to compete with them as an equal. I don't want concessions. But I also know I have different skills and abilities than most men, some of which may in fact give me advantages over my male colleagues. So I also want to be treated like the unique employee and team member that I am, which includes having the opportunities that fit my femininity well. I don't just want the "everyday feminism" argument that says all people should be the same, I want to treat everyone (and be treated by everyone) based on their own traits regardless of gender.

Unfortunately, my experience in the legal industry has rarely involved either equal or equitable treatment. In fact, most of my life I have been very aware of my gender—both how to use it to my advantage and how it works against me.

I remember as a girl in primary school, maybe in about grade 4, I sat in front of the mirror for hours. I would pull various faces, and tried various expressions on my face. I was testing what I looked like, and would tell myself never to do certain expressions because they weren't becoming. I practiced the smile I would use for photographs. I was hyper-aware at such a young age of how I presented to the world. This is when I first began to develop my mask, to hide who I really am from the world and present what's necessary to be accepted.

By the time I was the only female, at the age of 27 years, on an executive board of middle-aged men, my mask was fully developed. I would use my quiet voice and my smile to manipulate my way to being heard. I don't like confrontation, so I taught my face to make a poker face and my voice to be monotone. I was considered calm and cold, whilst inside I was a quivering, crying little girl, terrified I would be discovered. My calm exterior would often buy me the time I needed to think things over before I responded. My monotone voice would hide the emotional cracking in my throat.

Why did I feel like I had to contort myself into this machine to be accepted? I achieved far more than many of those executive men, because I knew how to talk to people and had great intuition with them. Yet, despite my achievements, I was paid significantly less than the men, and I had the extreme feelings of being an imposter. I felt like I didn't belong at that table. But the main reason I didn't belong at that table was because of their toxic behaviour; nothing to do with me.

Now I own my own business, one I started in the hope that I could conduct business on my own terms and in line with my values. But every day I still find I have to put on my mask. The legal industry in which I work is adversarial and based around professional men personally attacking each other for the benefit of their clients. I can't see how that can really achieve anything except resentment and bitterness. I'm sure some men and women can write it off as part of "the game", but I think the majority of us are going along with it because it seems to be the way things are done.

The more women who can get into high positions within large organisations, the better the business world will be. But that's not so simple as it sounds. There are many women who try that world, experience executive teams of men like I did, and decide not to put themselves through it again. Other women prefer to run their own small businesses, and/or work in smaller environments with other women.

The problem is that women's businesses, and women working with women, also don't promote equity or even equality, because men are often excluded. Creating an opposite situation like that, especially out of fear or anger, isn't equality, it's retaliation. These female leaders need to remember that they were scared girls too once, and help other women to follow in their footsteps while welcoming men in the spirit of equity. Just because they achieve success in a world dominated by middle-aged men, doesn't mean they can treat anyone—male or female—the way they may have been treated., instead of being blocks to the success of other women and holding their own gender to a higher standard that men. Susan Bulkeley Butler says that today's CEOs must have a strategy to achieve equality for men and women. This includes equitable policies, making a concerted effort to recruit women professionals, and creating a pipeline for women to ensure there are ample female candidates for all leadership positions when they become available. Applying equality and equitable principles is the next step for the feminist movement, one that both women and men can learn to embrace.

Role Models

I believe that gender should not be as big a deal as it is. Individual personalities aside, the qualities that make a great woman are usually also the qualities that make a great man. But because being bold and groundbreaking are typically considered "male" qualities, women are conditioned to be meek and patient and wait for someone else to break ground for them. This is a major reason that great female role models are so important...and also so scarce.

There are many highly intelligent and highly educated women in the world. Many are running businesses or achieving great successes in other areas. Yet the majority of household names that are considered 'successful' are men - Steve Jobs, Richard Branson, Warren Buffett, Elon Musk. Oprah might be the exception, and even she was an entertainer before she became a business owner.

The successful women held up as role models for other women typically work in more female industries, such as fashion and beauty. Think of Beyonce, Coco Chanel, Julia Child, Meryl Streep, even Mother Teresa—all are or were forces of nature, but in industries where women were expected or allowed to have a larger presence. The majority of famous women today are famous for how they look, or whatever issue they use their looks to draw attention to, not what they've achieved with their minds or skills. And when a woman does reach a high-level appointment, award, honour, or recognition in a male-dominated industry (from tech startups to film direction to politics), the celebration of that achievement always seems to come with an undertone of surprise that, frankly, makes me cringe. It's past time for the roll call of female role models to expand to a broader range of industries and backgrounds.

Despite being told how far feminism has come, we are usually told this by older white men, as if they have made a concession and they are condescending about it. We are still years away from true equality, and the role models that the media keeps presenting to our young women does not help us advance.

This issue is probably a chicken-or-the-egg argument in many ways, as there are many women who could put themselves forward as a role model but haven't, and there are many great women who have put themselves forward but do not get the attention they deserve. There are many successful businesswomen who are putting themselves forward with their books, bios, workshops and speaking, for instance. But as long as the mainstream media clings to the idea that female success looks like beauty rather than brains, and presents that idea (and only that idea) to young women watching, those young women who don't live up to that idea will be disappointed and dissatisfied.

Tom Basile said it well in saying what his daughter should look for in a role model:

A strong sense of right and wrong (yes, there is such a thing), someone who tells the truth (that's a big one), helps others, takes risks for the greater good, is humble without being meek, righteous without arrogance, and deeply generous, compassionate and reliable. Role models are forthright about mistakes and careful not to be hypocritical. They live what they preach, set high expectations for themselves and also hold others to high standards, understanding that people do falter from time to time. Above all else they live a life of purpose – as should you. Role models don't have to be presidents or CEOs. They can be ordinary people who commit themselves to living extraordinary lives. They often live for others.

Interestingly, this definition can apply just as easily to a male role model than a female one…and problematically, if his quote appeared without context, many readers might assume Tom was talking about a male role model. Even tougher to swallow is the fact that while male role models fitting this description do appear in mainstream media with some frequency, Tom's daughter will need to consciously take it upon herself to find female role models like this one. They will not be placed before her in the movies or on TV.

These role models for girls may be closer to home, like a teacher, local community leader or mentor.

Young women are influenced by a variety of adults and their peers, and there are a substantial number of studies that demonstrate that humans learn by modelling the behaviour of others, especially during childhood and teenage years. Clearly, negative role models during this time can guide and develop the mind and behaviour of a young woman to negative or undesirable traits—and positive ones can do the opposite.

True role models are those that possess the qualities that we would like to have, and those who affect us in a way that makes us want to be a better person. But positive female role models also need to be found to be modelled by young women, and if young women are not searching for them, then they are not likely to be put forward by the mainstream media. The media still celebrates women in more traditional roles, or roles that are more superficial, and if young women cannot live up to them then this can perpetuate a feeling of disappointment in themselves.

Violence

Women have come a long way in the corporate world, but for many it has been a hard road. The majority of physical violence at home is perpetrated by men against women. And while awareness of domestic violence has been increasing, awareness of workplace violence—which is also largely done by men—is not nearly as high. The truth is that women have had to put up with violence in the workforce for years: mental and emotional abuse, verbal abuse, or physical abuse.

Mentally and emotionally, men can diminish a woman's capabilities and achievements in the work place with various comments, body language or other undermining behaviours. Verbal abuse usually involves name calling and yelling, but ultimately is designed to affect the woman mentally and emotionally, as with more subversive versions of mental and emotional abuse to erode confidence.

At the worst, physical abuse also happens in the workplace. I once worked in an organisation where the management believed in motivating the workforce by fear and violence, both verbal and physical. As a professional woman, sitting on the executive staff, answerable only to the General Counsel, I expected to be treated professionally and respectfully. But I was slapped by a senior member of that executive team when I challenged him on an opinion he was expressing. This is the same team who degraded my every achievement by implying that I offered sexual favours to achieve my successes.

The slap wasn't so much painful as it was demoralising. I felt for a long time that I had brought it on myself, that I deserved it somehow. As an intellectual woman, I told myself that there was absolutely no need or excuse for that kind of behaviour, but another part of my mind said, "but if only I had stopped pushing my point ..." I didn't report it—I haven't even spoken about it until now— because I wanted to prove I was tough enough to cope with it myself and, at the time, take responsibility for my mistakes. I know now that such behaviour wasn't acceptable at all, for any reason, and I no longer hold any respect for the person who did it. But it took me years to get to that point.

As if the emotional cost weren't enough, a KPMG study estimated that domestic violence costs Australia $13.6 billion each year (*National Plan to Reduce Violence Against Women and Their Children,* KPMG 2012). I can only assume that this figure constitutes reported domestic violence, unless there was a rounding up based on an estimate of how many incidents of violence go unreported. Further, this report constitutes domestic violence, not violence in the workplace. So the financial cost of violence against women is economically significant, too! It's sad for me to think that financial costs may be the only thing that can get men's attention about this issue, but as long as they wake up, I'll take it.

Ultimately, women should not have to relate and "fit in" when that means accepting violent or sexually inappropriate actions in a professional setting. This behaviour is automatically exclusionary to women. The man's world needs to alter to allow women into it on an equitable basis, and the work place is no longer the place for violence in any form.

It's no wonder that women are dissatisfied with their careers and professional achievements when they are disrespected, even attacked, and their confidence is consciously eroded by their colleagues. Yet when women can find a supportive environment in which to work, they thrive and can find tremendous fulfilment.

'I think the best role models for women are people who are fruitfully and confidently themselves, who bring light into the world.'

- Meryl Streep

PART TWO: SYMPTOMS OF DISSATISFACTION

Dissatisfaction, and the pain that some of its symptoms cause, are not yours alone to feel. As we women talk to each other, we begin to understand how dissatisfied many of us are, whether it be with our home life, our work life, the many roles we feel we have to play, and/or the way society views and treats us. Our dissatisfaction is influenced by a myriad of variables, and demonstrates itself in our behaviours and personalities in a myriad of ways. Realising that many of us are dissatisfied, and that we are all suffer in our own ways, can be one of the most powerful antidotes to personal feelings of dissatisfaction and allow you to take some action towards change

Recognise that while life's difficulties are not always your fault or responsibility, you always have control over how you react to them. Once you know the symptoms of dissatisfaction, you can recognise them in yourself, and you can begin to address them and avoid taking out a lifetime membership in the cult.

In this Part, we will explore the symptoms of being in the cult of dissatisfaction, which include a deep belief that you're not enough as you are and must become someone else to be accepted, stress and anxiety from internal and perceived external (social) pressures, and lacking confidence and self-esteem. As we explore each symptom, we will touch on small ways to manage them, but Part Three will deal with these solutions in more detail.

'Shame is the intensely painful feeling that we are unworthy of love and belonging.'
- Brene Brown PhD

4 NOT BEING ENOUGH

Dissatisfaction, particularly with ourselves, often stems from a deep feeling that we are not good enough. We feel that nothing we ever do it quite enough, and that we are not beautiful enough or qualified enough to be putting ourselves forward. We feel like there's something missing in us when we compare ourselves to others, we feel like a fraud sometimes in our roles because we don't feel like we know what we're doing, or as women we subconsciously feel inferior.

When we can't meet our emotional needs directly, we develop strategies to satisfy those needs with substitutes. One such strategy might be driving ourselves relentlessly to make money or have power over others. We might desperately pursue sexual conquests. Or we might feel compelled to be helpful and of service; someone needed by others. We may try to meet our emotional needs with more immediate pleasures of food, alcohol or drugs. When they "work", these strategies provide immediate gratification through a quick surge of pleasure. But they also numb or cover our real pain and shame, our feelings on not being enough.

The overeating, the people pleasing, the power games, and the indulgences are easy to justify. We often say that they help us feel like ourselves or enjoy being ourselves in the moment. But because these tactics don't generally address our deeper emotional needs, rather than healing our suffering they merely replace it with dependence. This leads into a downward spiral that stick us even more firmly in the cult of dissatisfaction, sometimes now with an addiction that makes us feel even more dissatisfied than before.

Then, when our carefully constructed lives fall apart, we torture and berate ourselves with stories about how we are failures, what we could have done better, how no one cares about us. This response, of course, only digs us deeper. Distracted by our judgments of ourselves, we are not even able to recognise the raw pain of our emotions and the deep belief that who we are is not enough.

The thing is, this belief is false. You *are* enough. You have the skills and resources within you to achieve what you want. The deeper components of not feeling adequate include guilt and shame, suffering from imposter syndrome, and feeling a sense of inferiority due to your gender. These are symptoms of the cult of dissatisfaction, and they can be conquered.

Guilt and Shame

Guilt and shame are a cycle that we go around and around, over and over again in our minds, when we are dissatisfied. We tell ourselves that we shouldn't feel dissatisfied, and we feel ashamed that we do. We tell ourselves that we have so much to be grateful for, we don't deserve to feel dissatisfied because there are many in the world worse off than us, and then feel guilty for feeling ashamed and dissatisfied when all we have are "first world problems." We might even get a little angry with ourselves, and then put a forced smile on our face and get on with it…only to feel dissatisfied again before long.

I have been on this cycle many times, for many reasons. Usually, my dissatisfaction has been with my performance, either academically or work-related, but sometimes with fitness too. I often feel unworthy and lacking in some aspect, and then ashamed of myself. But the first major example of dissatisfaction leading to shame in my life was my self-image.

I first remember being dissatisfied with my body when I was going through puberty. I had been dissatisfied with some things about my appearance before this, such as my nose, my hair, my clothes, and my skin. But I became deeply ashamed of my body when I was about twelve or thirteen.

I was so ashamed of my new shape - of my growing breasts and curving hips - that I wanted to make myself as asexual as possible. I wanted my breasts to shrink, and my limbs to be as long and willowy as possible. I wanted to eliminate the curves as much as I could. Within a year, I had developed an eating disorder, which included overexercise, periods of fasting, some binging, and some purging. I measured my progress by weighing myself mostly, but also by measuring the tightness of certain clothes, measuring the span of my thighs against my hand span, and measuring the size of my waist by circling it with my hands.

I was also deeply ashamed of being noticed in or for my new shape, and cringed under the unsought-after glance or comment from anyone of the opposite sex. Any poor boy or man trying to offer a compliment was cut down with the lash of my angry tongue. I then felt incredible guilt for lashing out, and for the anger that I projected to the world. As my shame over my body was mixed with guilt for my behaviour, I became deeply dissatisfied with who I actually was. I did not believe that I deserved to eat. I began actively hating myself and soon became self-destructive. I engaged in even more risky behaviours than before, such as excessive alcohol consumption and self-harm. It took me years to undo the damage I did to myself during this downward spiral.

This is an extreme example of dissatisfaction and shame, but teenagers and their emotional reactions are often extreme. Body dissatisfaction, shame and anxiety of physical appearance is something that many women deal with regularly, especially young women. The media often makes this worse, portraying certain body types, colouring, fashion, style, height and traits as ideal.

But this form of dissatisfaction and shame is very focused on the physical and superficial aspects of ourselves. Shame often goes much deeper. Our dissatisfaction with ourselves leads us to a feeling that we are unworthy of love and belonging – that no one would want to talk to us, to have a coffee with us, to be our friend, let alone love us intimately.

This symptom of dissatisfaction can be so deeply crippling, that trying to shift the feeling of dissatisfaction may be far too overwhelming to deal with alone. You may need to seek professional help from a psychologist before anything else can be addressed. But remember that you are not alone in your feelings, and that satisfaction is not out of your reach.

Imposter Syndrome

The majority of you reading this book will be high achievers. You are professionals, career women, business owners, and highly educated. But for some of you, the more you learn, the more you realise you don't know. The higher you climb, the more you look over your shoulder. You wonder if you are good enough, or if you really know what you are doing, and you fell guilty for some of your success putting it down to luck.

Achievers like me and you have a constant need for attainment, and it pushes us to do more and achieve more. We often brush praise off for our achievements, because our motivation lies in striving towards the next goal on the horizon. We don't stop to celebrate our successes; we are always looking ahead.

Imposter syndrome is all this and more. Because at the same time, we also have a persistent fear of being exposed as a "fraud". It is a constant battle, because we are our own worst critics. We know our faults and flaws and issues and lucky breaks, even if the rest of the world doesn't, and we fear that one day they'll all find out.

I am a lawyer and a business owner, and I am constantly thinking that I'm not good enough or qualified enough, and someone is going to discover this about me. This has driven me to do course after degree after certificate, building up my credentials higher and higher every year. It also causes me to doubt myself as soon as another solicitor attacks my advice or position on a matter, even though disagreement and debate are the nature of the legal industry. I also often feel like I'm still a girl, just playing "business" and "house". Somehow I don't feel like it is all real, and that everything can be taken from me in a moment.

Imposter syndrome comes from the negative self-talk that is going around and around in your own mind. You have increased your expectations to that of perfection - you want perfection from yourself, from your work, from your life, and from your staff or colleagues. It is fine to have high standards, but you are allowed to make mistakes and be imperfect. And the perfection that you expect from yourself is often much, much higher than the good performance that others expect from you.

By realising that others have lower expectations of you than you have of yourself, you should be able to be more realistic about what you actually need to achieve. For example, if you expect that you can have a spotless clean house, work 60+ hours per week and also go to the gym every day to have a perfect body, then you are probably being too hard on yourself. Aside from the fact that you probably won't have time to do all those things—or at least do them all well—your idea of perfection isn't realistic. Your house can't always be the image from a magazine, working that hard over time can burn you out, and your idea of a perfect body might not be your spouse's idea of your perfect body.

Also, when you are trapped in your own self-talk, you are actually being very selfish. (This can be a way of breaking you out of the cycle, because as a perfectionist, you don't want to be selfish!) Instead of focusing on yourself, you can focus on your customers or clients or those you are trying to serve. For example, if you are giving a presentation, instead of focusing on whether you say 'um' too much or how you appear, you can try to focus on giving your audience the valuable information that they need and will appreciate.

Imposter syndrome can lead us to try to be or appear to be more or better than we are, letting us believe that if our audience thinks we're that good, we might actually become that good. The problem is, this actually sets us up for being found out as a fraud! So don't go there. When you are transparent about what you know, what experience and education you have, and what your background is, then you are setting the expectations of your clients and audience. Do not try to be someone you're not, or pretend you know about something you don't. It's better to honestly not know something than to make up an answer and actually appear fraudulent. If you are honestly providing valuable information that you have experience and education about, then you have nothing to worry about. No one expects you to know everything, unless you make out that you do know everything. You can be confident in what you know without coming across as obnoxious, because you know when to admit "I don't know, but I can help you find out".

Now, to start getting rid of the negative self-talk. Look at your life and acknowledge how far you have come. You have achieved a lot, and there are many people who would consider that you are a success. Make sure to celebrate your successes, especially the small successes you might normally brush off. When you get those top 5 things done on your to-do list, why don't you stop and celebrate instead of just filling up those spots on your list with new things? After you celebrate, you can refill your list, but at least acknowledge that you've just achieved a great deal by doing what you've already done.

What those with imposter syndrome need to tell themselves (including me) is to allow yourself to accept some praise occasionally for what you have achieved, and don't just put your achievements down to having "gotten lucky". You create your own luck by what you do, so accept that it is your achievement and celebrate it!

As a high achiever, you won't like being wrong or making mistakes, and this can increase your feeling of imposter syndrome. Don't let making occasional mistakes, which everyone does, tempt you into a negativity bias (where you think the bad always outweighs the good, even though the bad is usually 10% or less of what happens). Everyone makes mistakes occasionally, and you should focus on all the things that have gone well. Being wrong occasionally doesn't make you a fake.

Finally, understand that what you're suffering from is actually because you are a high achiever. It is a positive thing to be a high achiever, because you are equipped to work harder and longer than others. You can celebrate this! True imposters don't feel imposter syndrome, so by default, you can't be an imposter! Know yourself, take regular breaks, take time to celebrate successes, and limit your commitments to tasks that are aligned with your highest priorities. Also remember that nobody really knows everything, and most people are faking it at least some of the time— so if you stay true to yourself, you're already less of an impostor than most of the people you know.

Sexism and Inferiority

Dissatisfaction for women can stem from the real and perceived limitations placed on us because of our gender. Gender roles very much influence how we think and behave. As women, we often feel compelled to be submissive, to be meek, to be controlled. If we speak up, we have to be careful that we aren't labelled as "aggressive" or as a "bitch", whereas men are encouraged to be controlling and aggressive. We often curtail our true selves so we don't offend those in control (the middle-aged white men we talked about earlier) by breaking the gender stereotypes they're used to.

Slowly, the gender roles will change, as generations pass. But until that time, women need to find a way to be empowered by their gender, instead of dissatisfied with its limitations. These limitations are not always perpetuated by men either. Be aware that many gender limitations are imposed by other women, sometimes older or your peers, for even on yourself. Make sure you're not imposing gender bias on other women yourself.

The inferiority of women has pervaded for centuries, primarily because physicality equalled power when war and labour determined economy and success. Men's natural physical strength made them better suited to both fighting and farming, and over the years this grew into a sense of natural male superiority. Now that the agricultural and industrial ages have passed, and we have moved into an intellectual age, women don't need to compete with men by their physical strength. Women can compete as equals intellectually.

But because the transition from industrial age to intellectual age has occurred relatively slowly, over the period of thirty or forty years, we have a couple of generations that have experienced both periods and some of the gender roles that were standard for our grandparents but outdated now are still unnecessarily upheld. More and more women in generation Y and younger generations will become engineers, IT professionals, mathematicians and scientists, and other roles that have typically been seen as male roles.

The true change will also occur when men from generation Y and younger become industry leaders and the executives on boards of large companies— and welcome their female counterparts in those same roles. These men's views are far more equal and equitable than those of previous generations, and most of them acknowledge that women have the same intellectual capacity as men. Until then, women will often feel dissatisfied with treatment they receive based on residual ideas and attitudes.

Dissatisfaction also arises when we are doing the same job as men, if not more, and are paid less. The gender pay gap is real, and we should be dissatisfied with it. But we should also do something about it. Women in their twenties are generally paid the same as men, and are on the same track as men professionally. Then, a recent Visier analysis confirms, that when women hit their thirties and forties, they are not promoted into management positions like their male counterparts. Their professional progression stalls, maybe due to taking time off for children or changed priorities, but this is where the gender pay gap accelerates and never closes. Even when women reach management and leadership positions later in their careers, they are not paid equally for the same work.

What women cannot and must not do –is believe the old idea that we are fundamentally inferior to men. Women performed a vital but vulnerable role in society in times past when life was much harder than it is now. We needed to be protected, and we needed to have as many children as possible to bring forth the next generation of labour. But these conditions don't apply any more.

Maybe we can feel dissatisfied that the feminist movement has not done a complete job. We are able to work and vote, but general equality has still not been achieved, because of the gender roles that we are still raised with. But feeling that dissatisfaction doesn't mean we stop pushing for that last degree of change that is required.

Do not let anyone make you feel inferior due to being a woman. You know better than that, and whilst you may be conscious of having to comply with some gender stereotypes, such as being soft spoken, do it knowing that your achievements will be equal, if not greater, than those of your male counterparts.

'Society, being codified by man, decrees that woman is inferior; she can do away with this inferiority only by destroying the male's superiority.'

- Simone de Beauvoir

5 WEARING A MASK

In the previous chapters, I introduced the concept of wearing a mask. As a woman, I wear a mask to be part of a business world that was built by men. As a lawyer, I wear a mask of distant professionalism to convey strength and confidence. As a boss, I wear a mask so that my staff don't know the fear and anxiety that is boiling through my body. As a member of society, I wear a mask to avoid being teased, ignored or rejected. Wearing a mask is a symptom of dissatisfaction with myself and with how I think I need to appear to others to be successful.

Until recently, I had become so caught up in my assumed identity, that as a stressed, striving and potentially deficient person underneath, I had to wear the mask all the time. I was so caught up in my own stories in my head, that I was losing myself. I would sometimes spend days being impatient and judgmental towards myself and those around me. But I became aware of how dissatisfying this assumed identity was, and began exploring again who I really am and what I actually want.

Putting on masks begins with the assumption that we must change ourselves to belong. That's how I felt. I didn't that who I was, was enough. I couldn't be myself and be accepted or successful. I needed to be admired, but my insecurities about not being good enough were such that I had to pretend to be someone else. Since I was working as a lawyer, I learned and assumed traits that I believed successful lawyers required. I spent nearly two decades of my life trying to be who I thought the legal industry wanted me to be.

The process I went through to wake up from the dissatisfaction and take control of my life was about getting real with who I really am. I was worried that I had lost myself with all the masks I had been wearing. I was worried the masks would never come off, or that I would just be a shell underneath.

What if you and I could actually accept life - accept ourselves - for how we are?

"We can't hate ourselves into a version of ourselves we can love."

- Lori Deschene

Flawed and not enough

The predominant reason why women wear masks, and this relates back to feelings of shame and inferiority, is a deep belief that they are flawed and not enough. There is a lot of pressure to "stack up" in our culture. We feel as if there is something wrong with us, for example, if we are still single by a certain age, if we don't make a certain amount of income, if we don't have a large social circle, if we don't get a certain amount of Likes on our social media posts, or we don't look and act in a certain way in the presence of others. We beat ourselves up and don't feel good enough.

Unfortunately, in these situations we fear success almost as much as failure. If we fail, we prove to ourselves that we are flawed and not good enough. But if we succeed, we feel like an imposter like we talked about last chapter, like someone will discover us and take everything away from us.

Even after my Master's degree and further education and ten years of professional work, I still often feel that I am not a good enough lawyer. I fear that don't know enough to give considered legal advice. I also often analyse my interviewing technique and information gathering, and feel like I did not do enough to find out complete facts. I also feel flawed as a female lawyer - that I am not worth as much, that my time is not as valuable, and that I need to service cheaper clients as a form of social contribution. You may feel similarly about aspects of your career, or your femininity within it.

If our sense of who we are is defined by feelings of neediness and insecurity, we forget that we are also curious, humorous and caring—not to mention talented, skilled, and capable. We forget to experience life. I was so insecure about who I was, what I had to offer, and what I was doing as a lawyer that I lost myself. I couldn't laugh, I couldn't relax, I couldn't enjoy things, and I was not really living. I had created an anxiety-filled black hole of life for myself. Nothing I had to offer was good enough. I didn't feel like I could put myself forward as an expert. I didn't feel like anyone would want to work with me. I kept feeling that if I just did this or that, or one more course, or attended one more workshop, or wore something different, or had hair or makeup a particular way, or was a certain weight … So I changed how I dressed, how I wore my hair, how I reacted emotionally, controlled my facial expressions, changed my voice, and constantly lied about my age (I never felt old enough).

Wearing a mask can perform a valuable function, particularly as a woman in a business world. There is still the need to create good first impressions, remain calm and dispassionate during tough moments, and avoid oversharing with those who don't care about or respect you, and cultivating a mask can help with all of those. The problem arises when that mask becomes so effective that you lose yourself. When the mask stays on too long, you forget who you really are and your personal values. You start to believe that if you ever showed your real self and took the mask off, that people would not accept you and you would lose whatever credibility you established.

I have heard a few women, on various podcasts and TV shows, who describe not truly feeling like they could be themselves until they reached their fifties or sixties, because at that age they finally ceased to care what other people thought. Until that age, they were driven by what they thought society wanted them to do, and they cared more about what their parents wanted them to do and their husbands, and their community. This is one of the worst tragedies in modern times, that it can take six decades for a woman can feel the freedom to be themselves.

I believe I am currently in that journey of self-discovery, but in my thirties. I don't want to want another three decades to remove the masks. And I don't want you to wait that long, either. I am already worried that I have fundamentally altered who I am because I have been conforming and fitting in for so long. But I know it isn't too late—for me or for you.

Identities bound to professional lives

Women take on many roles - wife, mother, sister, daughter, and professional. Whilst men seem to be able to integrate their roles more effectively with who they are, often women become defined by their roles and get lost. Sometimes they can only identify who they are if they reference themselves to their husband or their children. Other times they feel their identity is bound to a professional role, especially one from which they get no fulfilment. Either way, it can be frustratingly easy for a woman to lose herself in her role.

As in previous chapters, I speak from experience. My identity has been so bound up with the fact that I am a lawyer, that I spent a lot of time who I am. Whenever people asked me what I did, in a networking or other context, I would cringe before telling people that I was a lawyer. I even began to tell people I was a business owner instead, but then they would ask me what my business was and I'd have to tell them it was a law firm. There was no escaping! They automatically made assumptions about me as a person because of my profession. They judged me based on various attitudes they had about lawyers in the community, and from TV, and from all the jokes about lawyers. They also held me in a bit of awe, so I could see them wondering what they could talk to me about. Surprisingly, a lot of people then thought of me a bit like the police and would always shy away from telling stories that bordered on breaking the law. Other times people felt compelled to share their legal issues and ask for free advice, assuming the area of law that I practiced in or that all lawyers know all legal issues. They didn't do these things maliciously, of course, but I hated the control my professional role had over my identity, so I didn't want anything to do with them.

As a woman without children, I have also lost friends after they've had children. We have grown apart because it seems to me that all the new mother could think and talk about was their baby, and then their toddler, and then their new baby, and then their brood of kids. I no longer had anything to talk about with these women, because I felt that they had become defined by their role as a mother. I knew there was nothing necessarily wrong with that, but I wondered when they will find themselves again. I felt bad for not being interested in their lives anymore. And I'm sure some of them felt similarly toward me, wondering when this woman was going to stop burying herself in a law career and find herself.

Being bound up in our professional identity can be hard to maintain as well. If everything depends on maintaining a brilliant career, and something goes wrong in that career, then your value and purpose as a person is suddenly in danger. In maintaining the image, your enjoyment is tainted by anxiety about keeping what you have and/or compulsively trying to get more. Maybe the risk is worth it, if your career fulfils you and it is your passion. But if your work doesn't satisfy you, then it's far too easy to become dissatisfied with yourself and your life as a whole.

It is easy to feel that something bad will happen if we don't maintain vigilance. We think ahead, plan out scenarios, think of the worst case scenario, judge other people and ourselves, and rarely live in the moment because we are so in our own heads. This is the very habit that keeps us trapped.

Very rarely have I been in the present moment, and I blame this for my bad memory, because whatever I am doing, I am always thinking about the next thing or planning tomorrow, or planning the right way to say the next thing in my head. Whilst this still has a place in business, because we have to plan and strive and think strategically, we also have to enjoy the process.

The difference seems to be understanding that you are *you*, and not what you do.

Ordinary or small lives

Much of our dissatisfaction arises because we are trying to be someone else - wearing a mask, embodying a profession, or thinking that who we are is not enough. We are striving for something more than we are or have, often because we are scared that we are not special and we will not have an amazing life. We are fearful of having an ordinary or small life.

But if your definition of "ordinary" or "small" is something less than a celebrity or tycoon lifestyle like you see on TV, you're looking at it from a really bad angle. If you compared yourself and your life to someone in a third world country, then you would be very pleased and may even feel guilty, because your ordinary and small life would seem like the lap of luxury to them. So realise that even though your life may feel small and ordinary, and likely could be better in many ways, it doesn't have to be larger-than-life and luxurious to be happy and meaningful. If you can live a simple, stoic, regular life and keep a perspective of gratitude and self-improvement, you can be happier than anyone you see on TV. If you want help with this perspective, consider a holiday or volunteer trip in a third world country every year or two.

Many meaningful causes and campaigns grow out of grassroots beginnings. If you take on the philosophy that if you improve one life in a small way each day, and everyone did that also, then the world would be a far better place, even if the one life in question is your own. Small things do make a difference, and a so-called "small" life can in fact be a very satisfying one.

Ignoring your passion is slow suicide. Never ignore what your heart pumps for. Mould your career around your lifestyle, nor your lifestyle around your career.'

- Raw for Beauty

6 STRESS AND ANXIETY

In the eyes of the world, I am highly functional. But internally, I am anxious, driven by fear, and often depressed. This is not clinically diagnosed, and I would never dare to talk to a doctor about this, because I am worried that I would get a label and be placed on medication. Whilst my brain is sometimes my worst enemy, it is also my greatest asset, and I fundamentally believe that I cannot have it altered by medications or drugs of any type.

Given my desire to avoid medication, my driven pace and habitual controlling in my daily life have become ways to cope instead. And they work well enough…but they certainly cannot be seen as thriving. When I feel anxious, the anxiety attaches itself to whatever is going on most immediate in my life. I might be stuck in a long line at the supermarket checkout counter, afraid I'm not going to get everything else done because I'm wasting precious time. I might have the early symptoms of a flu and worry that if it gets worse I'll have to cancel clients or miss work. This is a very dissatisfying way to live.

Many of us do this to some degree, whether to avoid medication or simply to feel a greater degree of control or a lower degree of stress. In business, we often head into emotionally charged confrontations nervously rehearsing and strategising what we will say. The more we fear failure, the more frenetically our bodies and minds work. We fill our days with continual movement: mental planning and worrying, habitual talking, fixing, scratching, adjusting, phoning, snacking, discarding, buying, looking in the mirror. When we are anxious, our moment-to-moment experience becomes one of constant reaction. We spend more time and energy defending our life than actually living it.

Yet these days it seems that busyness and overwork is applauded. We are socially rewarded for driving ourselves by anxiety, working ourselves into the ground, striving ever harder to prove to society that we are worthwhile at the cost of our peace of mind. Robbed of that peace, our minds too become trapped in rigid patterns: something terrible is about to happen to me; I am powerless; I am alone; I need to do something to save myself. Our minds urgently seek to control the situation by finding the cause of any problem. We point our finger at either others or ourselves.

It can be a vicious cycle. As a tense bundle of muscle, we often don't even recognise our own tension, let alone have any ability to relax it. The anxiety feels like such a familiar part of who we are. But we must recognise what this stress and anxiety that we live with daily is doing to us, how we create it ourselves in our own minds, and how many of the circumstances we fear may never actually arise.

As I researched anxiety for this chapter, I have also come to realise that my own reluctance to acknowledge my level of anxiety is because of social stigma. I do not want to be labeled as officially having anxiety, and I do not want medication because of my own belief that taking medication means weakness. But what I have also learnt is that many women operate in an ever-present state of low anxiety or worry, just like me. We may call it generalised anxiety for lack of a more official term, but it can blossom into episodes of full-blown panic attacks, phobias, or more specific anxiety disorders.

In the past, anxiety symptoms were dismissed as character flaws (think of the terms "worry wart", "head case" and "control freak"), and you were expected just to live with them, or occasionally medicate when they became so severe you couldn't function. I still have residual beliefs saying exactly that. But the truth is that telling women to silently suffer through anxiety is just as terrible as telling them that drugs are the only remedy for anxiety and panic attacks. Neither is correct.

Women's bodies

There are substantial discrepancies in how stress impacts women's health as compared to men's. Studies have found that women differ from men not only in their emotional responses to stress, but also in that acute and chronic stress may take a greater toll on women's physical and mental health.

When reacting to stressors, the body releases hormones such as cortisol, which causes a temporary increase in energy production, sometimes at the cost of other bodily process not required for immediate survival, such as digestion and immune system function. In women, these hormone changes and temporary process shutdowns lead to short- and long-term health problems much more often than in men.

Women are twice as likely to experience depression as men, and elevated levels of cortisol resulting from chronic stress (like that of a long-term, low-grade job or a sudden difficult life event like death or divorce) can act as a trigger for depression. And that's just one example.

Most of us know the feeling of tossing and turning at night, thinking over the events of the day or problems at work. Unsurprisingly, stress is a common cause of insomnia, which can in turn lead to difficulty concentrating, irritability and lack of motivation. When we are tired, we do not perform at our peak, and our mood is fragile and tends to swing from one extreme to the other. Also, when we're tired, we tend to eat more to get the energy that our brain feels that we need.

Stress can lead to insomnia, which can lead to overeating. But even if you are still sleeping well, stress can cause weight gain due to hormonal imbalances. Research has linked higher levels of cortisol to a lower waist-to-hip ratio in women (i.e. more weight around the belly area), as well as a decreased metabolism. High stress levels are also correlated with increased sugar cravings, which can lead to weight gain.

"A healthy woman has many wishes; an unhealthy woman has but one wish"

  - unknown

I had bad acne during puberty, from about the age of twelve years, and as a woman in my mid-thirties, I still have the occasional breakout. This was highly frustrating until I tied these breakouts to stress, and then they were predictable. Raised levels of cortisol in the body can cause excess oil production that contributes to the development of acne breakouts. A good skincare routine is helpful, but cannot completely protect against the effects of stress.

It gets worse. Not only are you tired, moody, gaining weight, and having acne breakouts, but stress can also cause hair loss! Significant emotional or psychological stress can cause a physiological imbalance which contributes to hair loss. Stress can disrupt the life cycle of the hair, causing it to go into its falling-out stage earlier than it should. While you may not notice hair loss during or immediately following a period of stress, the changes can occur three to six months later.

Prolonged stress can greatly impact the digestive system by increasing stomach acid, causing indigestion and discomfort, and in some cases contributing to the development of irritable bowel syndrome and ulcers. You might have been thinking you were developing some food sensitivities, but in fact it could just be stress. Reducing stress is key to maintaining a healthy digestive system, according to womenshealth.gov.

Then, stress can affect what fundamentally makes us a woman - our reproductive system. Acute and chronic stress can fundamentally alter the body's hormone balance, which can lead to missed, late or irregular periods. Researchers have also found that women in stressful jobs are at a 50 percent higher risk for short cycle length (less than 24 days) than women who do not work in high-stress positions.

Stress can also reduce sex drive, which should not be a surprise to any of us because it's the last thing we want when we are tired and stressed out. But this reduced sex drive can be the first sign of a more serious effect on our fertility. Elevated levels of cortisol suppress the body's natural sex hormones. While further research is needed to better clarify the link between stress and fertility, recent studies have found that women with high levels of alpha-amylase, an enzyme linked to stress, had a more difficult time getting pregnant. Women with the highest concentration of the enzyme during their menstrual cycle were 12 percent less likely to conceive than women with the lowest concentration of alpha-amylase.

So it's much more vital for women to manage their

stress levels! Be aware of what you put yourself through and what you allow the world to put you through, so you can do more to prevent chronic stress-related illness. Please, look after your body. Avoiding stress is easier said than done, but make sure you are doing as much as you can to rid your body of stress at the end of each day, and you support your health as much as possible.

Burn Out

There's stress, and then there's the next level: burnout, where you're working so hard for so long that you're just exhausted and your health starts to suffer. Burnout goes beyond chronic stress, because it may or may not be mental. Usually burnout refers more to doing too much physically, fitting too much into your life, burning the candle at both ends, and working yourself into the ground.

"We are in unprecedented times in terms of the global, always-on organisations," author and former Google program manager Jenny Blake told *Fast Company*. "Work comes in at all hours, and it can be hard to create boundaries that keep it contained and allow for proper rest and renewal." On top of that, women are expected (fairly or not) to serve double duty, taking care of the home and our relationships as well as professional duties. Also according to *Fast Company*, burnout also stems from young women being unhappy at work and feeling lost, while being pushed to work ever harder. In other words, we are trying to push through our dissatisfaction by doing all the things that we are told "successful" people do.

Of course, I am guilty of this too. I get up at 5am most days, to fit in an hour of exercise and set my mindset up with some journalling and affirmations. Then I get to work by 8am (if not earlier) and work until 6:30pm (if not later). I get home to make dinner, do some washing, sometimes go to the gym on the way home first, sometimes squeeze in a waxing or myotherapy appointment, then do the dishes, and sit back down to the computer by 8:30pm. Doing this daily is exhausting, and yet I and so many other women live schedules like this for months or years at a time. I can't imagine what it would be like if I had kids! Mothers are amazing - they fit far more into their days.

Professional drivers, depending on the laws in their industry and jurisdiction, must typically rest 60 minutes every 10 hours, or take 7 hours off after 12 hours straight. These laws, called "fatigue management legislation," were put in place to save lives on the road, and a few other industries have them as well—usually ones involving handling machinery or other potentially dangerous equipment. But in office-centric fields like law and business, fatigue management laws are nonexistent. In a woman's home life? Don't make me laugh.

It's not just in our days that we overwork, it's in our weeks and months and years. We put high expectations on ourselves to achieve immense goals in a short amount of time, and yet we don't give ourselves the benefit of time and patience for our achievements to develop themselves. We want achievement, recognition and credibility now, not in three more decades' time, and we work ever harder to make it happen. Sadly, whether we achieve it or not, most of us burn out in the effort and can't truly enjoy whatever success we attain. And if it does take us three decades…we probably won't last that long.

Psychologist Barbara White describes four broad career stages that women pass through as follows:

1. Early career development
2. Early 30s transition
3. Settling down — Late 30s transition
4. Achievement and maintenance

In their late 20's and early 30's, many women have left their personal lives and self-care in the dust because they are busy being busy and driven in their careers and hope to find some sense of balance in their overwhelmed lives. In addition, many women want to build long-term relationships and start families during this time.

In their late 30's and beyond, other women burn out realising that they've devoted many years to a career that is no longer fulfilling and are looking to find more meaning and purpose. This might mean re-crafting an existing job, finding vitality again through a hobby, or changing careers altogether.

Many men burn out too, but there's a difference. There are actually three dimensions to burnout: exhaustion, cynicism, and inefficacy (that is, weakness or helplessness). Men and women both experience all three, but they tend to go through them in different orders. Women tend to experience exhaustion first, followed by cynicism, then inefficacy — whey they get exhausted, they don't think they are being effective at work or at home so they stop work to evaluate. Men, on the other hand, tend to experience cynicism first, then exhaustion, and many of the men in the study kept working through both these stages because they didn't feel as though the symptoms from the first two stages impacted their quality of work. They didn't reach the inefficacy stage until they literally fell over, because they thought they were still being effective. Women are far more mindful and tend to look inwards during all stage of their career.

Even though we tend to be more self-aware, women are also generally more selfless than men. We think of everyone else first - our clients, our colleagues, our children, our husbands. We don't want to let anyone down. Whilst men and women can both be "givers", women tend to fall within a subset of "givers" called "selfless givers", according to Dr Adam Grant's research.

Part of our solution might be to change how we give. "Selfless givers" give their time and energy without regard to their own needs (hey — it's 3:00 p.m. and I haven't eaten yet today!). Selfless giving, in the absence of recovery, becomes overwhelming and can drive burnout. "Otherish givers" (another subset of givers), however, find a way to balance giving with their own self-interest and self-care. As you probably guessed, selfless givers are more likely to burn out. So if women could learn how to better balance their own and others' interests whilst still being compassionate givers, we would see less burn out.

Social Pressures

We live in a world that teaches girls to judge their

worth based on looks rather than abilities. In addition, girls get the mixed message that they should be themselves, but be perfect too. There are expectations that girls will be just the right mix of sporty, pretty, popular and smart. Girls pick this up, and double the pressure in their own minds. All this happens before the girls grow up into women, so as they grow, the pressure grows with them.

Social pressure is a psychological pressure based on society and other people's expectations. Wearing the mask I have spoken about previously is part of this, as is not feeling good enough in comparison to what we believe we should be. How women react to the social pressures they feel depends on each woman's needs, choices, values, and priorities.

If a woman is intellectual, they may value independence and self-reliance and therefore distance themselves from groups of women, appearing aloof but powerful and confident. If a woman is creative, they may value thriftiness and therefore adopt the appearance of the struggling artist. If a woman is maternal, they will often value their family and local community and will prioritise meeting with other mothers and volunteering to improve the experience of the community's children. If a woman is insecure, they may value a feeling of being needed and the security that a powerful man may provide, and therefore seek out a relationship above other needs or goals. And when women feel some or all of these concurrently, as some women do, the pressures overlap and combine exponentially.

The social pressures placed on women to be perfect mothers, as well as perfect housewives, are outdated, because there are so many more aspects to our lives now. Yet in many cultures, the social pressures include expectations that women not move out of these traditional roles. In many areas and cultures it is still expected that women marry by a certain age and have children straight away.

In cultures where women are more privileged and have access to equal education and a professional career, there are still expectations that they also fulfill the main roles within the household and caring roles for children, and sick or elderly family members. The gender biases of low expectations of women prevail, and the biases that women are not as ambitious as men because they prioritise other roles are also outdated. Whilst traditional and caring roles are vital and valuable, women are capable of doing more and being more if that is their choice.

Gender bias against women is often expressed through language and traditional gender beliefs that are quite unsuitable, especially at work. The blatant phrases such as "You, women", "You don't know what you are saying", "Stupid", and "You are as stupid as a cow" are hardly ever heard at work, whilst these statements are very often used by many families and are generally accepted in the home. Social pressures in the home, through biases and language can hold women back.

There are behaviours and language that were once acceptable in the workplace that are no longer acceptable. Likewise, what we used to find acceptable in the home can no longer be so. We are raising the next generation, and respect for both genders must be the core of all cultural values. Traditional gender roles can be chosen, but should not be forced on us via social pressure..

Intellectual and professional women are privileged in a sense, and we cannot forget that there are many women who have not even had the chances that we have had. That is to say, to raise awareness on gender equality even amongst women, is still a long and tough battle. Issues preventing gender equality include aspects of mentality, and deeply traditional ingrained beliefs and ideas about women's roles which are maintained through social pressures on women to fulfill. Many industries and cultures are slow to consider the economic benefits of the development of women intellectuals, and their participation in business and politics. Instead, women continue to have heavy societal pressures placed on them which are no longer relevant or important in modern society.

The reason why we struggle with insecurity is because we compare our behind the scenes with everyone else's highlight reel.'

-Steven Furtick

7 LACK OF SELF-CONFIDENCE AND SELF-ESTEEM

I am sure you can say that you are proud of yourself, on some level, or in some aspect of your life. I sure you can also come up with things that you like about yourself, too. But for many women it is more acceptable to talk about what they don't like about themselves, and to feel like they cannot prompt themselves and their strengths.

Self-esteem is an inner confidence, when a woman feels good about herself, because she already knows she's fine just the way she is. She is confident and aware of her strengths and abilities. She is also aware of areas needing work and growth. But that's ok because she knows she's not perfect (no one is), but she doesn't dwell on her weaknesses.

Lack of confidence and self-esteem is the biggest reason that we live in dissatisfaction and mediocrity. Self-esteem is essential for a healthy core identity issue, and our ability to experience joy. Once achieved, it comes from the inside out. But it can be assaulted or stunted from the outside world. A woman with low self-esteem does not feel good about herself because she has absorbed negative messages about women from the culture and/or relationships with family or loved ones. When a woman has low self-esteem, she loses control over her life and can become trapped.

With the reign of youth, skinniness, and perfect selfies on social media women often feel doomed to fail to live up to the images they compare themselves to. Then in the workplace, women who lack confidence tend to be self-deprecating, to minimize their accomplishments, or let others take credit for their work. They never move up. They end up going where they don't want to go, with people they don't want to go with. Again, out of control and trapped.

The truth about poor self-esteem is that the same doubt you are feeling might live behind the aloofness or arrogance, busyness or defensiveness, impatience or arrogance, that you notice in others. When you remember that others people feel the same kind of insecurity that you do, the same lack of confidence occasionally, then it's not like you're bad any more - you're just human. Your self-esteem and confidence can be changed.

Comparison

Long before Pinterest and Instagram, women were comparing themselves to each other. Girls began with magazines, and women progressed to a broader social comparison: mothers at the school gate, wives at social events, and a multitude of other roles and places. We see other women and put them into a super breed of magical women who have careers, maintain beautiful homes, patiently parent, create home-cooked meals (with vegetables that their kids will actually eat), and even go to the gym. No matter how hard we try, when we compare ourselves to others, we are always, in some way, falling short.

Comparisons are unhealthy for you, your mental health, and your relationships with those around you. If you feel like you're not living up to your comparisons with your colleagues or mentors, then you may cultivate jealousy and resentment towards them. We project perfection onto women we compare ourselves to, without actually knowing what's going on in their lives. We assume they have it all together, but actually they could be looking back at you thinking that you have it all together too.

We feel like we are under pressure to compete with each other, to get ahead, to stand out as intelligent, attractive, capable, powerful, wealthy. Someone is always keeping score (apparently). This does build jealously and resentment, and unfortunately women can be our own worst enemies. Instead of forming a sister-hood and helping each other, we compete with each other and want to brutally take each other down.

Long before Pinterest and Instagram (and even before the Internet), Leon Festinger proposed his "social comparison" theory in 1954. He argued that human beings have an innate desire to evaluate our own abilities and performance. In the absence of objective information about our performance, we will compare ourselves to others to see how we stack up. Decades of research have provided support for this theory. Given that our modern, complex lives don't provide much objective feedback about how we're managing work, family and other responsibilities, we're stuck relying on others to judge ourselves. But, the comparison process can backfire and cause us to judge ourselves unnecessarily harshly, particularly when we are comparing ourselves to the filtered, perfect images we see on social media — the images women seem particularly drawn to. Perhaps research suggesting that women's identities are more strongly defined by relationships to others than men's may provide insight as to why social media is so compelling to us into potentially harmful comparisons.

Comparison can make our own self-image much more fragile. It can trigger dissatisfaction with certain aspects of our lives and our abilities, and in turn trigger a sense of shame about being needy and undeserving, shame about being self-indulgent. When we compare, we are looking for something wrong with us. Especially when things seem to be falling apart, we compare ourselves to others who seem not to be, and we become painfully bound by the experience that something is wrong with us.

Unfortunately, the edict, "stop comparing yourself to others," is unlikely to be an effective recommendation to avoid this trap. Rather than fight the inevitable comparisons, there are ways that women can be thoughtful and proactive about the comparisons they make that are less likely to lead to dissatisfaction, frustration and perfectionism. A lot of this comes down to having some perspective, knowing how you define success, and getting comfortable with accepting who you are.

It is hard to feel good about yourself when you perceive that everyone around you is younger, prettier, skinner, smarter, wealthier, more successful, a better mum, or in a better relationship. But this script in our head is controlled by us, and we are making ourselves feel not good enough and deflating our self-esteem. Really, you don't know what other women are going through, so we should support each other and celebrate each other's success. That other woman you are admiring might be going through a hard patch in her marriage, or be struggling with infertility, or be in the midst of anxiety and depression, or be caring for a family member with cancer. Some perspective and compassion in comparison helps.

No one has the same combination of education, experience and natural talent that you have. Everyone has come from different backgrounds and circumstances, and has faced different trials to arrive where they are. You cannot make direct comparisons about yourself and others in every aspect of your life, because you do not know what is really going on in their lives or what they've been through or done.

'Owning our story and loving ourselves through that process is the bravest thing we will ever do.'

- Brene Brown

Self-Worth

Self-worth is another term for self-esteem, but I consider self-esteem to be more general about how a woman feels about themselves. Self-worth is more about one's sense of their own value or worth to society, in whatever role they are considering. Some women may have a great self-worth when it comes to parenting and homemaking, but find themselves feeling they are low value in the workforce. Or vice versa. When we feel unworthy, we find proof of our inadequacy everywhere we look.

Feeling unworthy goes hand in hand with feeling separate from others. If we are defective, how can we possibly belong? The more deficient we feel, the more separate and vulnerable we feel. Underneath our fear of being flawed is a more primal fear that something is wrong with life, that something bad is going to happen. Our reaction to this fear is to feel blame, even hatred, towards whatever we consider the source of the problem: ourselves, others, life itself.

Our feelings of unworthiness and alienation from others gives rise to various forms of suffering. The most glaring form of suffering being addiction. It may be to alcohol or food, or drugs. For some it may be a relationship. Or some try to feel important through long hours of gruelling work - an addiction that our culture and many industries often applaud.

My identity was based on pleasing others and the fear of not being liked or valued if I didn't. To manage feeling inadequate, I would embark in one self-improvement project after another, trying to feel worthy. I would hold back and play it safe rather than risk failure, and I would keep extremely busy. I became my own worst critic so no one else could think worse of me than "me", and I focused on other people's faults to make myself feel better. I took on a "me versus the world" or an "us versus them" attitude, and couldn't trust anyone.

The belief that we are deficient and unworthy makes it difficult to trust that we are truly loved or appreciated. Work becomes an indirect way of trying to win love and respect. We might find what we do entirely meaningless, we might hate or resent our job, yet still hitch our desire for approval and connection to how well we perform. We may tell ourselves "I have to do more to be ok".

We want to feel "good enough" all the time in our work, parenting, relationships, health, appearance, and life. We want others to be a certain way - always happy, healthy, loving and respectful towards us. Yet because these things don't happen, we are driven by the feeling that something is missing or wrong.

Our most regularly used strategies to get what we want also become a defining part of our sense of self. The overeating, the competing, the people pleasing; all this feels like "me". When I feel insecure, producing is my most readily accessible strategy for feeling worthwhile - whether it's emailing, finishing a draft legal document, paying a stack of bills, or having a clean house. This producing is not simply the natural urge to be creative and contribute to the mix of life, it is energised by fears of inadequacy and the need to prove myself. The price is that I become more speedy, impatient and distant from those I love. I get disconnected from my body as I relentlessly urge myself onward to get yet another thing done. Feeling self-centred and bad about myself for workaholism doesn't slow me down. "Getting one more thing out of the way" seems the most reliable way to get what I want - to feel better. I am fearful that without being productive, I will lose everything.

Like me, you might drive yourself relentlessly to be helpful and of service, someone needed by others. Or other strategies used to deal with a feeling of unworthiness include a compulsion to make money or have power over others. We might desperately pursue sexual conquests. We often try to satisfy our emotional needs with more immediately pleasures of food, alcohol and drugs. But because they don't genuinely address our needs, our suffering continues and with it our reliance on whatever provides pleasure or relief. This can create addiction; all because we feel a low sense of self-worth and insecurity in the woman that we are.

Fear of being a flawed person lay at the root of my addictive endless achieving, and I had sacrificed many moments over the years in trying to prove my worth, often to people I didn't really care about. We lose ourselves in thoughts about what is wrong, how long it will last, what we should do about it. We strive to tie up all the loose ends and to avoid making mistakes, even though we know both are impossible.

Feelings of low self-worth in any aspect of your life can lead to dissatisfaction with yourself as a woman. Predictably, women are also more likely to doubt themselves and experience feelings of low self-worth than men. Yet we also have incredible capacities for compassion and lifting other people up. If we can feel satisfaction in making others happy, we cannot doubt that feeling, and we can ultimately change our feelings of low self-worth. You have huge value to offer to your family, community, and to the world - what will it take for you to realise this?

'If you are trapped between your feelings and what other people think is right, always go with whatever makes you happy. Unless you want everybody to be happy, except you.'
   - unknown

Trapped

More often than not, when we talk about women feeling trapped, it is usually in a relationship that they cannot leave. But increasingly dissatisfaction can arise because a woman feels trapped in their job or broader circumstances, and does not feel like they have the control or power to make a change. Their lack of confidence, lack of resources to change, and poor self-esteem keeps them trapped, and they become deeply dissatisfied with their situation and themselves for not being able to change.

The report by The Work Foundation and Employers for Work-Life Balance, found that women were still 3.5 times more likely than men to perform all domestic tasks and over 12 times more likely to manage all childcare. The result was that they were often pulled in two directions at once and could end up trapped in lower paid jobs. The survey showed that the only time men and women shared tasks evenly was when their salaries and career priorities were equally matched.

We can feel trapped in our societal roles, we can feel trapped in situations due to debt, we can be trapped into our job due to lack of confidence to change, and we can be trapped in relationships due to habit. There are many situations that we can be trapped in, and for many reasons which usually come down to lack of confidence and self-esteem.

When we are trapped, we revert to a programming for survival. We can only read behaviours and opinions as signs of friend or foe. We cannot see people for who they really are, and we are more inclined to judge them on generalisations and misconceptions. If we relax, we have the capacity to enlarge our sense of belonging and connection. We can see behind appearances, see the vulnerability in others and realise that we are not alone - we do belong.

For nearly a decade, I have felt trapped. I have felt trapped on a career course without any means to redirect the path I was on. I felt trapped because I was worried about what other people thought of me, and because of what I thought society expected of me. These perceptions were wrong, and I couldn't see through them, because I was trapped. I began down the path of becoming a lawyer, got my degree, got my qualification, and then began following a fairly typical career path without any thought about what I actually wanted. By the time I paused to wonder what I wanted, it was nearly ten years later, and I hadn't enjoyed what I was doing for years.

I have also felt trapped due to debt, and still often

do. I have a certain amount of debt that needs to be serviced, and I like a certain amount of disposable income. Yet, my income only ever just covers the necessities. This feeling of being trapped in a career path, and being unable to change due to the debt I have, leaves me frustrated and dissatisfied. I feel separate and alone, I feel isolated and like I am in a straight-jacket. I feel like no one else could ever understand, and I feel deeply ashamed and embarrassed that I'm in this situation.

Many times have I whispered "oh please, oh please, give me strength", and now that I have started to share these feelings, I know that others often also ask the universe for help, strength and guidance. When we feel disconnected and afraid, we long for comfort and peace that come from belonging to something large and more powerful. This causes many to reach out, or reach deep within, in mediation or prayer.

Objectively, many societies, including Australia, have more freedom than ever before. However, the level of freedom that we enjoy, and the amount of information that we have access to, arguably seems to have eroded many of our freedoms subjectively. Subjectively it is easy to feel trapped by society. We do have a choice in whether to participate in popular culture, 24 hour offices, endless social media, body image and having the ideal home life. Sometimes it's hard to determine whether a decision we make is due to societal norms, or if it is actually want you want (like owning a smartphone or having a Facebook profile).

When we are feeling trapped, and caught in our own self-centred drama, everyone else serves as supporting cast, some as adversaries, some as allies, most as simply irrelevant. They become unreal and less human to us. Because we are so trapped in ourselves, we cannot pay close attention to anyone else, and those around us, even friends and family, become two-dimensional cardboard figures - not humans with wants and fears and hearts. If they become unreal to us, then we lose sight of how they hurt. Because we don't experience them as feeling begins any more, we not only ignore them, we can inflict pain on them without compunction. Hurting those we love is the last thing any of us actually want, but when we are scared and hurting ourselves we may not realise our effect on others.

When those closest to us become unreal to us, we might easily assume that we know what life is like for them and forget that, like us, they are always changing, their experience is always new. We lose sight of how fully they too are living with hurts and fears, and how hard life can be on the inside for everyone. We all have the capacity to change and grow, and we can all feel trapped in different situations throughout our lives. The key is to recognise when your dissatisfaction is due to a feeling of being trapped, develop skills to increase your confidence and self-esteem to make new decisions to change your situation.

PART THREE: FINDING SATISFACTION THROUGH CHANGE

Awareness is half the battle, and now you've explored the external cues of dissatisfaction and the symptoms that could manifest in you. So you're well equipped to escape the cult. But beware - the cult doesn't want to let you go! It will take some continual awareness on your part for a while, and a conscious effort to battle against the overwhelming dissatisfaction.

The word "resentment" means "to feel again". Each time we repeat to ourselves a story of how we've been wrong, we feel again in our body and mind the dissatisfaction of that experience. But often enough our resentment of others reflects our resentment of ourselves. So don't succumb to the cult again - retain your fresh sense of possibility that you have control of how you feel. You don't serve to suffer anymore, and you have the power to break that cycle in your life.

We aspire to do good in our society and community. We all belong to this world, and on some level we know that everything that happens within it affects everything else. Every thought we have, every action we take has an impact for good or for ill. You cannot contribute your best if you are dissatisfied, so if that is your true goal, you owe it to yourself and the world to overcome your dissatisfaction.

Here, I am now giving you the permission to be yourself, no matter what appears - burning rage, gnawing anxiety, cruel thoughts or utter despondency. It's all **you**, and it's not bad or wrong. I am also giving you permission to change if what shows up isn't what you want, to have a happy life and to be satisfied.

Part Three will now explore ways in which you can overcome many of the symptoms of dissatisfaction and learn to live with some of the external causes. With mindfulness and awareness of the causes and symptoms, you are better equipped not to fall back into the cult. As part of giving you permission to lead a happy life and to make changes, I will let you know what change **is not,** so that you can forgive yourself for wanting change and clear the path to make it happen. Once you have allowed yourself to believe that change is possible, we will focus on changing what you can control and letting go of what you can't. Finally, we will explore some of the deeper ways of dealing with the internal symptoms of dissatisfaction, so that you can find happiness through acceptance of yourself and what you have achieved.

'There are only two days in every year that nothing can be done. One is called yesterday and the other is called tomorrow, so today is the right day to love, believe, do and mostly to live.'

- Dalai Lama

8 WHAT CHANGE IS NOT

Everyone wants to be happy. Change can be anything you like - it's just doing things differently from how you're doing them now, or viewing things differently from how you're viewing them now. But there may be beliefs that are holding you back from changing, or because you think you can't change, but I am giving you permission to change your life now.

You may be considering a complete career change, like me, or you may just need to have a chat with your current employer about making a couple of changes that will make you happier. That could be working shorter hours, or only a few days a week instead of full time. You might try to negotiate a couple of forms working from home; the possibilities really are endless.

The change you want to create may also be in another area of your life than work and career. It may be where you live, it might be your relationships with friends or your spouse, it may be how you dress and act in certain situations, or it may just be allowing yourself to change your mind on certain issues.

Just because I've given you permission to change, and I am encouraging you to give yourself the same permission, change in itself doesn't just happen. We also must address the negative thoughts that stop us from changing. Wanting to do something that makes you happy is not resignation, it is not defining ourselves by limitations (being unable to be resilient), it not an excuse to withdraw, it is not a self-indulgence, it does not make us passive, it is not about accepting that we are "good" or "bad". Making changes that will make you happy and be more true to yourself will allow you to be a stronger woman.

Failure

Wanting change does not mean you have failed. If you stay in the negativity and let it define you, then allowed something outside yourself to define you. You need to define who you are. This is the only way you will find an escape from dissatisfaction. Define the true you and don't let anyone treat you in a way that makes you feel worthless. Think of all the good things that you have done, and let those good thoughts fill your heart.

Failure is often defined as a lack of success, but it can also be defined as being unable to do what you expected or wanted to do. With mini-disasters striking left and right, is it any wonder you might begin to think bad things about yourself? No matter how many hours you work, you can't get everything done on time. The lover who once made you smile now only seems to harp at you. Your family constantly points out how you are less than perfect. Even strangers can put you down. Posts on the internet or strangers on the street can take a verbal swipe at how you look or what you're doing.

Everywhere you look, there is someone pointing out what is wrong with you! Your looks don't measure up. Your career is not where you want it to be. Relationships fall apart around you. Family is a nightmare. Money is a problem. Nothing is the way it was supposed to be, and people are eager to let you know how you have disappointed them.

After hearing this over and over, too many people, especially women, start to believe that they are somehow flawed. You buy into the constant pecking, and you come to think that if everyone is saying that you are a failure, it must true, right? This final concession makes you your own worst enemy. You start apologising to yourself or anyone who might be listening for things that aren't your doing at all.

- You're sorry that you can't lose weight.
- You're sorry that your spouse had an affair.
- You're sorry that you haven't been able to do better at work.
- You're sorry that your children have done something wrong.
- You're sorry that you are sick and are not doing enough for your family.
- You're sorry that you married a man who hit you.
- You're sorry that you can't find a job.

Each of these and more feels like a personal failure, an effect of your own flaws.

I had been plagued by an endless feeling of running from failure for probably as long as I can remember. Primarily, it was schoolwork and then later it was any setback on the career path that stood before me. But I was also terrified of failing socially by being able to mingle with friends, and of failing to meet certain stereotypical expectations of marriage and children.

I've especially felt like I have failed as a woman because I've never become a mother, even though I know I don't want to become one. There are such strong expectations that I have children, because I am in a stable loving marriage. As soon as we married, there were questions about when we would have children. Ten years later, most people have given up asking, but I know they are thinking that I had better do it soon if I'm going to do it at all. I feel like a failure as a woman because I don't want to have children. I don't want to make the time in my life for them, and I don't want to be a guilt-ridden impatient mother (which I know I would be).

When I finally accepted within myself that I needed to change professions, because I am unhappy and will lead a dissatisfying life if I remain doing this work, I also felt deeply like I had failed. I felt like I was failing to meet the expectations that those around me had of me. I felt like I was failing my community and my clients. I felt like I was failing my profession, because I am good at the work, and lead with integrity.

I felt that because I was neglecting to do what was expected of me, even though I was choosing my own happiness instead, I was a failure.

Probably not surprisingly, the more I have spoken about my dissatisfaction, the more people have expressed that they don't actually have an expectation of me. They thought I was happy, so if I wasn't, they all accepted that I should do something different.

After much soul searching, I also realised within myself that I don't have to exit my profession fully. I can still offer a lot to the profession, and I have learnt so much from my years as a lawyer. I can do the aspects I enjoy, and I can still use my advocacy skills for areas I am passionate about, such as equality and gender issues.

When you start feeling like a professional failure, it can become extraordinarily easy to fixate on the idea that your career fate is totally out of your control, decided by forces far outside your own power. This kind of thinking is seductive because it provides a narrative that indulges all your darkest thoughts: not only does your life suck, but it was predestined to suck long before you were ever in a position to do anything about it, so there is literally nothing you can do now. But as seductive as it can be, it's not true. You can change, and you are not a failure for doing so. Your professional life is a marathon, not a sprint, and just because you tripped up or someone got a few seconds' head start on you, doesn't mean you're never going to catch up.

The important thing to remember is that your fears and worries about being behind or on the wrong path in your career don't isolate you; you're not the only person to feel this way. Don't feel like a failure for deciding that you made in mistake in choosing the career that you did. There's still plenty of time to make a change.

How can it be a failure to want to pursue something that will make you happy? I have not failed. Nor will you.

Defining ourselves by limitations

Defining ourselves by limitations is similar to considering yourself a failure, because you are defining yourself by something you perceive to be real but actually isn't. To change is to reject and break through what you may perceive as your limitations.

When I realised that I wanted to do something different, and that I was dissatisfied with my career, my first thought was that I was giving up. I didn't have the grit and resilience to stick it out. The legal profession often talks about building resilience as a mechanism to fight against mental health issues. I also thought that if I didn't demonstrate grit and perseverance in just continuing to do what I have always done, then I was failing.

We are constantly told that we must be resilient, we must persevere, and we must display grit and courage.

I have written about these traits myself:

> *When a woman is in the right path, she must persevere. I speak of this because there are some people who are "born tired;" naturally lazy and possessing no self-reliance and no perseverance. But they can cultivate these qualities.*

> *It is this grit and perseverance, this determination not to let the "blues" take possession of you, so as to make you relax your energies in the struggle for independence, which you must cultivate.*

> *How many have almost reached the goal of their ambition, but, losing faith in themselves, have relaxed their energies, and the golden prize has been lost forever.*

> *Perseverance is sometimes but another word for self-reliance. Many persons naturally look on the dark side of life, and borrow trouble. They are born so. Then they ask for advice, and they will be governed by*

one wind and blown by another, and cannot rely upon
themselves. Until you can get so that you can rely upon
yourself, you need not expect to succeed.

-Woman's Rules for Making Money

But change doesn't mean that you're not resilient, gritty or that you're giving up. We hear that the definition of insanity is sometimes described as doing the same thing over and over again, expecting a different result. So, the way I was applying resilience and grit to myself was that I had to persist, and wasn't allowed to change. By doing the same thing over and over again (practicing law) and expecting something to change (that I would suddenly start enjoying it), was really an insane thought on my part. Yet I also felt that if I didn't keep practicing law, then I wasn't resilient.

I have had to look at those traits closer, and I have realised that what I perceived as a limitation on my character was actually not. Grit and resilience are not contradictory traits that prevent change.

I have worked in the legal industry for over 10 years, despite a lot of difficulties and misery - that *does* demonstrate grit and resilience. I have persevered. But do I have to persevere until I have a breakdown? No. That is not perseverance; that is stubbornness and stupidity.

I have not stopped working - I am demonstrating grit and perseverance in following my dream. I am resilient because I have not given up, and I will continue to make things happen in my life instead of letting life happen to me. I was not allowing myself to change, because I falsely believed that there was something wrong with me if I wanted change; that I was weak and not gritty. But I had set that limitation on myself! No one else thought this of me, so I could give myself permission to change. You can change too - I give you permission!

Self-indulgence

The other thing that change is not, is that it is not a form of self-indulgence. Self-indulgence is often defined as the pursuit of pleasure. And yes, we are changing to make ourselves more happy, but we are not just seeking the easiest or most pleasant path. Making a change is not turning away from what's hard to find what is easy. It is not a decision to be passive - it is a conscious decision to pursue something different.

Self-indulgence to the extreme can have long term costs. We may find out, for instance, that what we've chosen to help make us feel better has damaged our lungs (e.g., nicotine), or our liver (e.g., alcohol). Or that our self-indulgent (or addictive) habit has—directly or indirectly—injured our most important relationship. Or that what we've done to get an adrenaline rush has left us in a body cast! Or we may learn that, as a result of poor food choices or binge eating, we've developed diabetes or heart disease. Or that the debts we've incurred from gambling, drugs or shopping are now overdue . . . and unpayable.

Contrary to what some people might assume, self-indulgent people are not particularly happy—even though they may *strive* for happiness (or at least the immediate "highs" of happiness) a good deal more than the rest of us.

I have struggled with feeling like I am being self-indulgent for wanting to be happy. I also struggled with the concept of "following your passion", because I believe that passion can be self-indulgent if it doesn't serve a larger goal. (Not to mention that following your passion can be a bad business and life strategy, if your passion is not viable.) I admit that I do sometimes still judge other women who have left the corporate world to run little craft, jewellery, or skin product businesses that they started based on passion. But who am I to judge them and their choices, especially when those passion businesses do serve greater goals for these women? I'm working on reducing these judgments.

This is how my mind works, though, and these are some of the negative beliefs that have held me back from making change. I don't want the same negative beliefs to hold you back. I thought writing was indulgent, and could not be financially viable, for a long time. But the more research I have done, and the more self-published people that I have found and followed, the more I realise that a tidy living can be made from writing.

I wondered if I was just being self-indulgent in wanting to be a writer, and turning away from a difficult profession to something easier. However, I know writing for a living will not be easy, and I want to work hard at it. The difficulty of each profession will just be different – instead of timelines and emotional stress imposed by clients, I will face other challenges of self-motivation and producing creatively. So, in the process of doing research for this book, I have come to accept that what I am actually doing is self-nurturing, not self-indulgence.

As opposed to self-indulgence, self-nurturance fosters both the physical and psychological health requisite to our happiness. Here we're not "treating" ourselves to something that briefly makes us feel better but ultimately is bad for us. We're not looking for a quick fix, an escape, or to drown out nagging doubts we have about ourselves. Rather, we're addressing our inherent desire to leave dissatisfaction behind through responsible action based on our long-term personal needs and priorities.

It can sometimes be easy to confuse self-indulgent and self-nurturing behaviour, since both are meant to address our deepest wants and needs, and both strive to make us happy on some level. For me, it came down to a feeling that I was unworthy of feeling happy and fulfilled. By trying to give myself happiness and fulfilment that I didn't think I deserved, I believed that I was being self-indulgent. But in reality, transitioning from law to writing was a self-nurturing step, and as I connected more deeply with my own worth, I began to see that more clearly.

We all deserve to be happy and fulfilled. We are worthy of those things, and pursuing them responsibly is not self-indulgence. As we begin to treat ourselves with more respect, love and compassion, nurturing ourselves rather than indulgent our whims, we will get closer to that happiness and fulfillment. We may feel anxious or guilty at first, as these practices go against all the negative messages and self-indulgent habits we've been living with for most of our lives, but the more we tell ourselves we are ready and worthy to commit to our own growth and happiness, the more positive and purposeful we will feel and the stronger progress we will make.

"You're the average of the five people you spend the most time with." - Jim Rohn

9 CHANGING WHAT YOU CAN CONTROL

Dissatisfaction often arises from a disconnect with our expectations for ourselves. This disconnect is either due to any number of the external causes which influence us, that we've discussed in Part One, including being sold the cultural myth, doing what other people expect of you, living within stereotypes, political correctness being imposed on us, working in a man's world, and a the type of role models that the media portrays. Or the disconnect could be due to internal symptoms of being not good enough, so we alter ourselves. It can also come from both trying to control things that are not within our ability to control, and failing to control the things that we can. There is no point worrying about things we cannot control, but there are many things that we can control that we often don't. We can control and change our expectations of ourselves, as we can change who we associate with, our thoughts, and how we react in certain situations. We can also control how and when we change ourselves—we don't have to lock ourselves into any idea, plan, habit, or thought pattern.

Don't forget that every person, including ourselves, is new to every single moment. People can change moment to moment, day to day, year to year. Don't lock others in, and don't lock yourself in.

In the previous chapter, I gave you permission to change. Now we will explore the areas of your life that you can control and change, so you can begin to reduce your dissatisfaction. You are firmly in the cult of dissatisfaction if you would prefer to do nothing and simply complain. But if you truly want to escape the cult, then you have the control to be able to achieve it.

Associations and Environments

Everyone is their own person, but research has shown that we're more affected by our environment than we think. The law of averages states that the result of any given situation will be the average of all outcomes affecting that situation. So our environment's effect on us is the average of everything we encounter within it. And when it comes to relationships, we are greatly influenced — whether we like it or not — by those closest to us.

If you want to change how dissatisfied you are with a certain area of your life, look at the people around you in that area of your life. For example, let's say you want to lose some weight and get fit. If a lot of your friends are overweight, and your social life involves eating with them frequently, then it will be really difficult for you to achieve weight loss. But if you bring a personal trainer into your life, and you reconnect with a couple of other friends who have active lifestyles which don't revolve around eating, then your change will be easier.

The cult of dissatisfaction can be infectious for exactly this reason. If your close group of friends tend to spend their time moping around, complaining about their situation, and wondering why things aren't just handed to them, then you might tend to do and feel the same way. But if you surround yourself with people who are energetic, motivated, and ambitious, then you may feel more of a drive to change and achieve your goals as well.

Likewise, if you are ambitious and have a lot that you want to achieve, then having unambitious, disorganised friends will not help you. You are likely to become frustrated by such friends anyway, particularly if they aren't interested in changing—even when you tell them about your desire to change and ask them to join and/or support you. These friends aren't bad people, and they likely still care about you. But if they are not making you stronger, and you are not having a positive influence on them, then they are only making you weaker. I encourage you to kindly but firmly step back from friends who will not support your efforts to change, and find other friends who will.

If locating and connecting with these people is difficult, there are other ways to design your environment to achieve a more positive effect. For me, I struggle to befriend women of my age in my community who have the same drive and ambition as I do, but I make up for that by listening to lots of business and mindset podcasts every week. This way, even if I can't associate with the kind of people I want to regularly, I can still train my mind to think and process and respond the way I want it to.

The other thing I have done more and more over the last couple of years is consciously focus on building a better network around myself, and using those new connections to help myself move in the professional directions that I want to. LinkedIn can be a good tool for this. As you strategically reach out to people, share content with people that you think they will find relevant, keep in touch regularly, and help your new connections meet their goals, you will build a network that wants to help you succeed.

As well as LinkedIn, I have joined more community and industry associations to get more exposure and give me a better chance of meeting people that I want in my life. I am also a member of a couple of networking groups for professional women, as well as a few online groups for similar communities. Groups like these can help you form further networks and meet likeminded people from around the world.

Finally, if you truly take Jim Rohn's quote to heart, make sure to look for people who have already done what you want to do, and who are already living how you want to live. Research them, read their books, read their content, listen to their interviews, and if you can, connect with them and reach out to them. In the end, they are real people, and you may be able to provide them with something valuable so that you can become part of their network.

One of the fastest ways to change anything in your life is by surrounding yourself with people who will not only support you, but who are already doing what you want to do, or living how you want to live. So make the conscious decision to examine those close people in the important areas of your life, and consider making some changes.

Thoughts

As well as those with whom you associate, you can also control your thoughts. The questions we ask ourselves, and the words we use when we think about things or about ourselves, determine a lot of our behaviours. Our mindset is the single biggest thing that we can change about ourselves—and doing so can get us the biggest results.

The secret to challenging your mindset is to start tuning in to the stories you're telling yourself. You see, our brains are sense-making machines. They love it when all the pieces of the puzzle fit together. And one of the ways we try to make sense of things is to tell ourselves stories about what's happening and what might happen next. Over time, these stories become beliefs that we hold. The problem is, most of the time these stories are not entirely correct.

Professor Carol Dweck has found that people with a fixed mindset believe intelligence and talent are hard wired and they were born with almost all the natural abilities they'll ever have. As a result, the research Dr Dweck has conducted suggests that people with a fixed mindset tend to avoid challenges, tend to be unwilling to be seen to be exerting too much effort, and feel threatened by negative feedback for fear that any failure will prove to others they're not really good enough and there's nothing they'll be able to do about it.

Unfortunately, because these people are very outcome focused, both success and failure cause anxiety for them. Failure in particular tends to induce a state of helplessness making it hard for them to learn from what's happening, causing them to disengage with the problem and eventually to give up. Now don't be misled by these descriptions, it's not that these people aren't capable of achieving great things.

Conversely, people with a growth mindset, Dr Dweck's work has found, believe they're born with the capacity to improve their intelligence and talents through learning and effort, and as a result, they tend to create learning goals around mastery and competence. We now know from neuroscience this is absolutely correct. When we believe our abilities are like muscles that can be built up with practice, we're more willing to take on new challenges, to put in our best efforts and to accept criticism, because we understand that learning is the only way to keep improving.

A growth mindset influences goal setting, achievement and motivation, ultimately determining feelings of self-belief, outcomes achieved and wellbeing. In fact, people with this mindset seem to reach ever higher levels of success in all domains of life.

Here's the thing: even if you seem to have a fixed mindset, you don't have to keep it or let it hold you down—as long as you're willing to change the way you think. For example, rather than just accepting a fixed mindset story, like "I'm not really good enough", you can challenge that story by asking the simple question "is that the only explanation?". Is "I'm not good enough" the only explanation of what might happen as I take this challenge on? Or perhaps, might I learn something new? And maybe, even if I don't pull it all off, could this be a great experience for me to have?

As you begin to challenge your stories, you'll notice the way you feel and what you're willing to do start to shift with each new story you create. By challenging our stories, we regain the power to choose beliefs that help us learn and grow and accomplish what we're truly capable of instead of automatically limiting ourselves. We also become more aware of the negative messages and stories we've been telling ourselves in the first place, which allows us to break vicious mental cycles and downward spirals more readily.

There are also specific mental practices we can adopt to help ourselves change our stories. Affirmations have certainly helped me with my mindset, and I have a few key affirmations that I say in the morning or throughout the day to keep my mood lifted and shape my beliefs in a positive direction. Over time, I have come to absolutely believe many of them. Some of my favourites include:

- My marriage is becoming stronger, deeper, and more stable every day.
- My body is healthy, my mind is brilliant.
- I am the architect of my life; I build its foundations and choose its contents.

Many people also have found that meditation helps their mindset. Because I am a restless person, I have not been able to adopt a meditation practice: however, I tend to use a long run as my meditation time. Doing a 10km run, or longer, completely sorts out the jumble in my brain, and I come away positive and clearer than before. Sometimes, I also do a guided meditation at the end of the day, to help me fall asleep.

Because how you think about yourself, how you think about situations, and how you think about life can have such a profound effect on your life, this is also where the greatest change can occur. So become aware of your thoughts and what you tell yourself, and start adopting some practices to change that conversation going on in your head.

Mentoring and coaching

Once you have accepted that if you want your life to change, and that you need to take control and change something, you may realise that you need some help. Yes, you can assess your associates yourself and make changes there. Yes, you can become mindful of your thoughts and try to change your mindset by yourself. But the truly successful people in the world have had help getting where they are. This help usually comes in the form of mentors, coaches, or accountability partners, or a combination of all three.

Mentors typically provide support and guidance for individual growth and maturity. Coaches are often more job-focused and performance oriented. Mentoring is specifically about you, not about performance objectives. Coaching is more impartial, more results-oriented.

A mentor is like a sounding board, they can give advice but the partners is free to pick and choose what they do. A coach is trying to direct a person to some end result; the person may choose how to get there, but the coach is strategically assessing and monitoring the progress and giving advice for effectiveness and efficiency.

Currently, I am part of a mentorship group run by a podcaster who became a personal mentor a while ago. We meet as a group fortnightly and also have regular one-on-one chats both with the mentor and with each other. I also have a personal business coach, as well as a speaking coach. I am working one-on-one with my business coach on a fortnightly basis to achieve specific goals within my legal business (mainly an exit strategy of either scaling, selling or merging). My speaking coach focuses on my individual profile, developing my intellectual property for my topics, and my goals for that venture.

I also have accountability partners that I met through the mentorship group that I speak to fortnightly, who are essentially peers with me on my journey to make big changes. We talk about our wins, and then our goals, and we make sure that each other achieves those things each fortnight that we set out to achieve. Some other accountability partners I have had over the years include gym-buddies and fitness training partners who have helped me stay motivated and achieve my fitness goals.

Periods when I have had mentors or coaches in my life have been when I have made the greatest personal and business gains. Most of my mentors and coaches have been paid, but you can engage mentors into informal relationships for free. Though building a free mentorship relationship with someone can take a lot of time and investment on your part to begin with, it can pay great dividends in time.

Some of the benefits of having a mentor include:

- knowledge and contacts - a combination of detailed industry knowledge and personal introductions to the mentor's contacts, which might not otherwise be readily available to you.

- business and life skills - valuable business and life skills, including best business practices, appropriate behaviours and protocols.

- perspective and vision - Discussions with your mentor will stretch your thinking by providing you with another perspective to your own, as well as the benefit of your mentor's vision, which comes from their wider experience.

• reduced feeling of isolation - a sense of peer partnership that might not otherwise be available to you within your organisation.

• wisdom and learning from past experiences - the lessons that your mentor has learned along the way through their past successes and failures.

• a sounding board - Having a good mentor will also enable you to test your ideas and discuss your points of view with an interested listener in a safe and confidential environment.

Change is possible alone, relationships with mentors and coaches can accelerate it greatly. Spending money on these programs is an investment in yourself, because your future will be bigger and brighter than without it. And if you are reluctant to jump straight into a paid arrangement, you may be surprised to find how many people are happy to have a chat with you for free. People are more willing to help you than you may think, because we really do want to see you succeed.

"Our lives improve only when we take chances and the first and most difficult risk we can take is to be honest with ourselves." ~Walter Anderson

10 HAPPINESS THROUGH ACCEPTANCE

When I say happiness, I don't mean that you're bouncing around laughing all the time (though if you're that kind of person, go ahead!). I mean that you are without anxiety and dissatisfaction; you are tranquil and calm, content and satisfied.

I believe that we can find happiness through acceptance. Not resignation to our circumstances, which leads to dissatisfaction. I mean a deeper acceptance of who you are, what you want in life and why. Also, an acceptance that change is possible, and a belief that you can find satisfaction.

As your trust deepens in yourself and the possibilities open to you, you will become better at expressing yourself what you want. Rather second-guessing yourself, rather than being paralysed by self-doubt, you can honour and respond to the promptings that arise from your intuition. When we are not consumed by guilt and shame, and no beating ourselves up by comparisons to others, we are free to cultivate our talents and gifts, to contribute them to the world in service. We can then be free to be happy, and be satisfied with the whole of life, without holding back.

Honesty and Authenticity (Realising Who You Are)

First and foremost, I want you to be honest with yourself. This is sometimes the hardest thing to do. Before we can accept ourselves, we need to be honest with who we actually are and what we want.

We spend our lives seeking something that is actually right inside us, and could be found if we would only stop and deepen our inward attention. But distracted, we spend our life on our way to somewhere else. We do what we think others expect of us, and we try to please people that we don't really care about.

Most people I know think I'm an honest person, and in general that's true. I am honest with many people, sometimes bluntly, sometimes gently. However, in the past, I have rarely been honest with the person who matters most—myself.

Here's the thing: I like hiding. I don't like spilling the beans about myself to a new friend, even if they've been a new friend for five years. I'm squeamish about social events, and if I can avoid the details of where I've been or what I've been doing, I will. I am adaptable - I can fit into most situations, and I adopt one of many of my masks to do so. As I have said before, I became so good at wearing masks that for a long time I didn't know where the masks stopped and where I truly began.

To get honest with myself, I had to find myself again under all those masks and the armour I had built to survive. I had to work out what I actually did and didn't like about where I was in my life. I had to work out what my values were and what my deep life principles were. I had to work out what I actually wanted to stand up for. I did most of this through journalling. Over time I realised that many of my preferences were actually other people's, and many of the things that I let slide I actually really didn't want to put up with any more.

I finally gave myself permission to give myself some attention; and attention is the most basic form of love. I paid attention to myself, and I actually think that I've found myself again. I have heard other women say that they waited decades to do this, and felt like they could never be truly themselves until they stopped caring what other people thought in their fifties or sixties. But I couldn't wait another twenty years until I was in my fifties to get honest, because I didn't want to be dissatisfied for another twenty years.

Getting honest with yourself is hard. If you're not used to being honest with yourself, you can't imagine just how hard it is when you start. The good news is that you'll probably only be able to dish it out in small doses, so you can get used to it over time. The first piece of brutal honesty I gave myself was this: you do not value yourself, so others don't value you either. Ouch! The next piece of honesty was that I have created the situation I was in myself, and I was the only one who could change it (that is, working 70 hours a week in my own business, doing work I didn't like, for far less money than I would be paid if I worked for someone else).

Most of us are deceiving ourselves in any number of ways every day. The work of getting honest with ourselves is the hard work that only we can do for ourselves (although a good psychologist could help).

As well as journalling, mentoring, and perhaps therapy, another thing that can help is to visualise who you want to be in five years and how your life is at that time. I have done this process in detail a number of times; once dot-pointing various aspects about my life in five years' time, and another time actually writing out a typical perfect day in detail, like a story.

I suggest you do this now: write out your typical perfect day, which is what you will aim to have in five years' time. Where do you wake up, and with whom? What does your house look like, how is it decorated, what's outside? What is your morning routine, how do you feel when you wake up to do it, and then what do you do throughout the day? As much detail as you can. This can really help you work out your goals, and keep you on track, because you won't say "yes" to things that won't lead you to this vision.

Values

Your values are the things that you believe are important in the way you live and work. They determine your priorities, and, deep down, they're probably the measures you use to tell if your life is turning out the way you want it to. Many of us actually haven't consciously worked out our values. So if we are dissatisfied, while we may know on some level we aren't living up to our values, we may not know what values we aren't living up to.

When the things that you do and the way you behave match your values, life is usually good - you're satisfied and content. But when these don't align with your personal values, that's when things feels … wrong. This can be a real source of unhappiness and dissatisfaction.

This is why making a conscious effort to identify your values is so important.

Life can be much easier when you acknowledge your values - and when you make plans and decisions that honour them. Because if you aren't clear on your personal values, then how can you figure out what you want really want? And how can you be sure that your actions are congruent with who you are at your core?

Most people have approximately 5-7 core values that identify who they are at their core. Each person's values are unique to that person; even if two people happen to pick the same value word, such as integrity, each person will demonstrate it differently in her daily actions and language.

If you value family, but you have to work 70-hour weeks in your job, will you feel internal stress and conflict? And if you don't value competition, and you work in a highly competitive sales environment, are you likely to be satisfied with your job?

I feel like I have been a mental and emotional chameleon throughout my teens and twenties, changing my viewpoints and values to match first those of my parents and then those of my peers and then those of my workplace and industry. Secretly, inside myself, I had my own dreams and opinions, ideas, and desires. Eventually I realised that in order to be happy, I needed to learn to live according to what *my* values were.

After some consideration, I determined my values include accountability, efficiency, competence, knowledge and education, and continuous improvement. These are the qualities I will not budge or compromise on. Looking at this list gives me a deep satisfaction calm, because if I can live by these values every day, in every decision that I make, I know I am living how I want to be living.

When you know your own values, you can use them to make decisions about how to live, and you'll be able to better determine the best direction for you and your life goals. Think of it as a tree: values are our roots that keep us grounded in what's important to us. The strength of the values determines the strength of the trunk, branches, leaves and fruit from year to year. A strong tree supports the ecosystem around it; a leader with strong values supports the organisational culture.

Appreciation

Gratitude almost seems like another buzz word at the moment, but there is something deeply effective in being grateful for what you have. Perhaps it is because it's hard to feel fear or anxiety whilst you are focusing on being grateful. In any event, being appreciative of what you have is my third aspect of finding happiness and satisfaction in your life and with who you are.

People who regularly practice gratitude experience more positive emotions, feel more alive, sleep better, express more compassion and kindness, and even have stronger immune systems. And gratitude doesn't need to be reserved only for momentous occasions: Sure, you might express gratitude after receiving a promotion at work, but you can also be thankful for something as simple as a delicious meal.

Appreciation for the great things in your life can put other things in perspective, since it can refocus your attention onto what is truly important and what you value most. Being grateful can also make us thankful for what we already have, rather than always looking outside ourselves for something more that we don't have.

Research by UC Davis psychologist Robert Emmons, author of *Thanks!: How the New Science of Gratitude Can Make You Happier,* shows that simply keeping a gratitude journal—regularly writing brief reflections on moments for which we're thankful—can significantly increase well-being and life satisfaction.

You'd think that just one of these findings is compelling enough to motivate one into action. But if you're anything like me, this motivation lasts about three days until writing in my gratitude journal every evening loses out to watching some drama on Netflix.

Here are a few keys I've discovered—and research supports—that help not only to start a gratitude practice, but to maintain it for the long haul:

- Don't confine yourself to a gratitude journal, but mix it up a bit. Sometimes I use a guided gratitude meditation, sometimes I write down what I'm grateful for, or sometimes I leave a little note for my husband about what I love about him;

- Be social about your gratitude practice, and share the love. Tell people "thank-you" for particular things, send a handwritten note or card, or send them a private message via social media;

- Make a game of noticing a couple of small things to be grateful for every day. Instead of just being grateful for your family, make it more specific - be grateful for something small they did for you or for a personality trait that you love.

"Be thankful for what you have; you'll end up having more. If you concentrate on what you don't have, you will never, ever have enough." - Oprah Winfrey

CONCLUSION

Now that you have reached this point, I truly hope that you feel you can create change in your life and escape the cult of dissatisfaction. I wanted to use my life, and my struggles, as a deep exploration of what is causing dissatisfaction amongst women today, as well as how we internalise dissatisfaction. I hope it has made you think, and perhaps encouraged you to have conversations about these issues with other women.

I do not have all the answers, but I know that awareness is half the battle against dissatisfaction. You are now aware of the external causes which can create dissatisfaction, which include cultural causes, a feeling that we have to do what's expected of us, having gender stereotypes imposed on us, and not feeling like we have the same rights and opportunities as men.

You are also aware now of the internal symptoms of dissatisfaction, because although you may have had a general feeling of unhappiness and wanting something else, we have learnt more deeply about what causes these feelings. We explored not feeling like we were ever enough, imposter syndrome, having to pretend to be someone other than ourselves, stress and anxiety, comparison, feeling trapped, and being fearful.

Then I shared with you what I have learnt to begin to address these symptoms within myself; giving myself permission to change, taking control of my life, and getting to know myself better. Yet I am also conscious that I have not given you practical steps to address the external causes of dissatisfaction.

I have not addressed how to deal with the cultural and gender issues that are external to us and over which we have little control. I didn't do these things because I can't do them. Unfortunately, I cannot provide a sweeping solution for dissatisfaction arising from larger cultural and gender issues. What I hoped to do instead was spark a conversation about these issues, and make us conscious of them. That is why I want you to focus on you, because when we turn to ourselves first we can make a change one person at a time.

As women, we cannot sit back and complain without doing anything, and we certainly cannot wait for equality to be handed to us by men. It is in our hands. Yet, we can only have control and influence over so much in our lives. I do not want to create more dissatisfaction by telling you that you can change the world, and then you will blame me when you fail. Rather, it will take many of us together to create deeper cultural change. As mothers, aunts, grandmothers, sisters, and wives, we all have the influence to change ourselves and our immediate family, though.

Look after yourself first, and then make sure that gender inequality and social pressures are not impacting those closest to you. Take care of other women within your influence. We can no longer abide women hating on other women. We must stand up for each other, make sure unacceptable and inappropriate comments or behaviours are not allowed. Question gender biases and assumptions, and no longer stand silently by.

When we change ourselves, we can then impact our immediate family and our close work colleagues, and then our broader community network. The more women who talk about these issues and have the difficult conversations, the more women will stand up for each other. We can create a groundswell of change that begins with ourselves. When we personally change and acknowledge our values and what we will and won't tolerate, we then impact a wider circle. The more of us who do this, the more communities we impact. The more communities we impact, the more towns and regions we impact, and we may even impact whole countries and the world if we don't give up. Be part of this ground swell movement for change, beginning with you first.

ABOUT THE AUTHOR

Jacqui Brauman is the principal solicitor at TBA Law and an Accredited Specialist in Wills and Estate. After beginning in rural public education, Jacqui has achieved a Bachelor of Laws, Bachelor of Accounting, Graduate Diploma in Tax Law, and Masters of Applied Law in Wills and Estates. Her career of over 10 years in the legal industry has taken her from Central Victoria to rural New South Wales, to Sydney, and back to the outskirts of Melbourne.

Jacqui is a member of the Law Institute of Victoria, the Society of Trust and Estate Practitioners, HerBusiness, Business in Heels, the UN Women National Committee Australia, and Professional Speakers Australia. She has written and published two legal books: *In Case of Emergency,* and *Death and Social Media;* as well as three ebooks for empowering women: *Steps to Success for Women, Acres of Diamonds,* and *Graduate the School of Hard Knocks.* She speaks and writes regularly on women's empowerment throughout Australia.

BIBLIOGRAPHY

10 Benefits of Having Good Mentors, Blue Sky Coaching, https://www.blueskycoaching.com.au/pdf/v4i11_mentors.pdf

Barr, Corbett, *What Is Lifestyle Design?*, Fizzle, https://fizzle.co/sparkline/what-is-lifestyle-design

Basile, Tom, *A Letter to My Daughter About Female Role Models*, Forbes, 11 August 2016, http://www.forbes.com/sites/thomasbasile/2016/08/11/a-letter-to-my-daughter-about-female-role-models/#6822780b1fc1

Bell, Christopher, *Bring On Female Superheros!*, TEDx Oct 2015, https://www.ted.com/talks/christopher_bell_bring_on_the_female_superheroes

Brach, Tara, *Radical Acceptance*, Random House Group Ltd, London 2003.

Brewer, Holler, *List of Gender Stereotypes*, Health Guidance http://www.healthguidance.org/entry/15910/1/List-of-Gender-Stereotypes.html

Bulkeley Butler, S., *Gender Equality = Men + Women Working Together*, Huffington Post 10/06/2014: http://www.huffingtonpost.com/susan-bulkeley-butler/gender-equality-men-women_b_5924828.html

Carpenter, Derrick, *The Science Behind Gratitude (And How It Can Change Your Life)*, Happify Daily, http://www.happify.com/hd/the-science-behind-gratitude/

Chan, Amanda, *10 Things That Can Lower Your Libido*, Huffington Post, 7 November 2011 http://www.huffingtonpost.com.au/entry/lower-libido-10-things_n_947297#s351166&title=Big_Life_Events

Clay, Kelly, *Why Millennial Woman Are Burning Out*, Fast Company, 3 August 2016, https://www.fastcompany.com/3057545/the-future-of-work/why-millennial-women-are-burning-out

Davis-Laack, Paula, *Will We Ever Let Girls By Good Enough?*, Psychology Today, 15 June 2015, https://www.psychologytoday.com/blog/pressure-proof/201206/will-we-ever-let-girls-be-good-enough

Davis-Laack, Paula, *Why More Women Are Burning Out in Their 20s and 30s*, Huffington Post, 1 June 2015, http://www.huffingtonpost.com/paula-davislaack/why-more-women-are-burnin_b_6417144.html

Eschenroeder, Kyle, 21 Proven Ways to Overcome Imposter Syndrome, Start Up Bros, http://startupbros.com/21-ways-overcome-impostor-syndrome/

Feller, Alison, If You're Approaching Burnout By 30, You're not Alone, Well Good, 10 March 2016, http://www.wellandgood.com/good-advice/millennial-women-burnout/

Gregoire, Caroline, 10 Ways Stress Affects Women's Health, Huffington Post, 23 December 2014 http://www.huffingtonpost.com.au/entry/health-effects-of-stress-women_n_2585625

Groth, Aimee, You're the Average of the 5 People You Spend the Most Time With, Business Insider Australia, 25 July 2012, http://www.businessinsider.com.au/jim-rohn-youre-the-average-of-the-five-people-you-spend-the-most-time-with-2012-7

Guest-Jelley, Anna, 4 Tips to Tell the Truth About Yourself and to Yourself, Tiny Buddha, 2011, http://tinybuddha.com/blog/4-tips-to-tell-the-truth-about-yourself-and-to-yourself/

Holiday, Ryan, 'Meditations on Strategy and Life', Projecting Rules, 25 August 2010 http://ryanholiday.net/projecting-rules/

Imposter Syndrome, Wikipedia: https://en.wikipedia.org/wiki/Impostor_syndrome

Kliff, Sarah, This Study Reveals Why the Gender Wage Gap Explodes When Women Hit Their 30s, Vox, 9 Sept 2016, http://www.vox.com/2016/9/9/12854718/gender-wage-gap-age

Kofoed, Mara, Stop Comparing Yourself to Others, A Blog About Love, 31 January 2012, http://www.ablogaboutlove.com/2012/01/how-to-stop-comparing-yourself-to.html

Loehr, Anne, How To Live With Purpose, Identity Your Values, and Improve Your Leadership, Huffington Post, 6 May 2014, http://www.huffingtonpost.com/anne-loehr/how-to-live-with-purpose-b_5187572.html

Marsh, Sarah, Young Women; Do You Feel the Pressure To Be Perfect?, The Guardian, 1 September 2016, https://www.theguardian.com/commentisfree/2016/sep/01/young-women-pressure-perfect-education-looks-work-relationships-social-media

McQuaid, Michelle, Afraid You're Not Good Enough?,

http://www.michellemcquaid.com/growth-mindset/

Moss, Gabrielle, 5 Things To Remember When You're Feeling Like a Failure, Bustle, 13 October 2015, https://www.bustle.com/articles/116391-5-things-to-remember-when-youre-feeling-like-a-failure

National Commission of Audit, 'Age Pension', Towards Responsible Government, 2014 http://www.ncoa.gov.au/report/phase-one/part-b/7-1-age-pension.html

National Plan to Reduce Violence Against Women and Their Children, Council of Australian Governments, KPMG, https://www.dss.gov.au/sites/default/files/documents/05_2012/national_plan.pdf

Papilio, Do People Feel Trapped in Today's Society?, Essential Baby forum, 27 February 2007 http://www.essentialbaby.com.au/forums/index.php?/topic/336375-do-people-feel-trapped-in-todays-society/

Pick, Marcelle, Anxiety and Worry in Women, Women to Women, https://www.womentowomen.com/emotions-anxiety-mood/anxiety-and-worry-in-women-causes-symptoms-and-natural-relief/

Price Mitchell PhD, M., How Role Models Influence Youth Strategies For Success, Roots of Action, 14 January 2014, http://www.rootsofaction.com/role-models-youth-strategies-success/

Richards, Carl, Learning to Deal with Imposter Syndrome, New York Times, http://www.nytimes.com/2015/10/26/your-money/learning-to-deal-with-the-impostor-syndrome.html?_r=2

Rowse, Darren, Strategies for Overcoming Imposter Syndrome, Problogger, http://problogger.com/podcast/121-2/

Schurman-Kauflin PhD, Deborah, You Are Not A Failure, Psychology Today, 27 August 2012, https://www.psychologytoday.com/blog/disturbed/201208/you-are-not-failure

Seltzer PhD, L.F., From Self-Indulgence to Self-Nurturing, Psychology Today, 8 June 2008, https://www.psychologytoday.com/blog/evolution-the-self/200806/self-indulgence-self-nurturing

Severance, Angela, Lifestyle Design: How To Create Your Life As You Want It, Tiny Buddha: http://tinybuddha.com/blog/lifestyle-design-how-to-create-your-life-as-you-want-it/

Sonnier, Madison, 7 Things to Remember When You Think You're Not Good Enough, Tiny Buddha, http://tinybuddha.com/blog/7-things-to-remember-when-you-think-youre-not-good-enough/

Smouse, Debra, **Determine What Will Make You Happy by Identifying Your Values**, Tiny Buddha, 2013, http://tinybuddha.com/blog/determine-what-will-make-you-happy-by-identifying-your-values/

Starcevich PhD, M.M., **Coach, Mentor: Is There a Difference?**, Centre for Coaching and Mentoring, http://www.coachingandmentoring.com/Articles/mentoring.html

Sun, Amy, **Equality is Not Enough: What the Classroom Has Taught Me About Justice**, Everyday Feminism, http://everydayfeminism.com/2014/09/equality-is-not-enough/

Sunderland, Marianne, **Attitudes of Entitlement: What are they and why should I care?**, Abundant Life, 9 January 2012: http://www.mariannesunderland.com/2012/01/09/attitudes-of-entitlement-what-are-they-and-why-should-i-care/

Tran Thi Minh Duc, Associate Professor, **Gender Bias and Social Pressures on Intellectual Women**, Hanoi National University, 26 June 2012, http://gas.hoasen.edu.vn/en/gas-page/gender-bias-and-social-pressure-intellectual-women

Vlazyn, Maggie, **Women and Self Esteem**, Psych Central, https://psychcentral.com/lib/women-and-self-esteem/

Warrell, Margie, **Afraid of Being 'Found Out'? How To Overcome Imposter Syndrome**, Forbes, http://www.forbes.com/sites/margiewarrell/2014/04/03/impostor-syndrome/#612abe74eb9d

Westring, Alyssa, **Why Women Should, And Can, Get Past the "Compare and Despair" On Social Media**, Huffington Post, 26 March 2014, http://www.huffingtonpost.com/alyssa-westring-phd/why-women-should-social-media_b_4655819.html

Working Women Feel Trapped, Daily Mail Online, http://www.dailymail.co.uk/news/article-183547/Working-women-feel-trapped.html

www.ingramcontent.com/pod-product-compliance
Lightning Source LLC
Chambersburg PA
CBHW021929190326
41519CB00009B/957